12/50

The Singapore Story

Noel Barber was born in Yorkshire in 1909 and educated mainly abroad. During the Second World War he served as a navigator with the RAF and was awarded the Légion d'honneur. He was for many years chief correspondent of the *Daily Mail*.

He is the author of twenty-seven books including two in Fontana, *Sinister Twilight* and *The War of the Running Dogs*, and, most recently, his autobiography *The Natives Were Friendly* (1977).

Noel Barber is married to an Italian, has two grown up children, and lives in Chelsea.

Noel Barber

The Singapore Story

From Raffles to Lee Kuan Yew

Fontana/Collins

First published by Fontana 1978
Copyright © Noel Barber 1978

Typeset by Northumberland Press Ltd,
Gateshead, Tyne and Wear

Made and printed in Great Britain by
William Collins Sons & Co. Ltd, Glasgow

Set in Intertype Baskerville

CONDITIONS OF SALE
This book is sold subject to the condition
that it shall not, by way of trade or otherwise,
be lent, resold, hired out or otherwise
circulated without the publisher's prior consent
in any form of binding or cover other than
that in which it is published and without a
similar condition including this condition being
imposed on the subsequent purchaser

For Gitte
with love

Contents

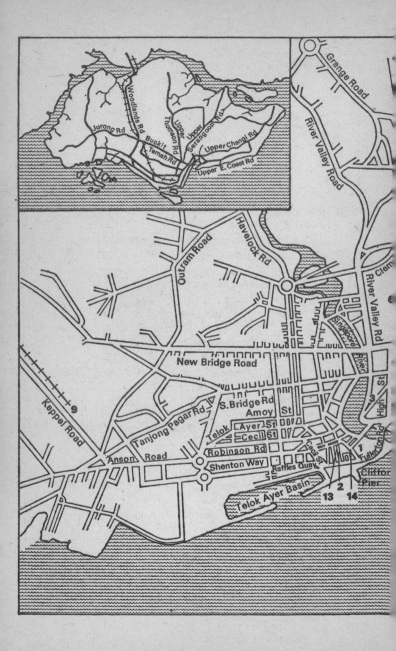

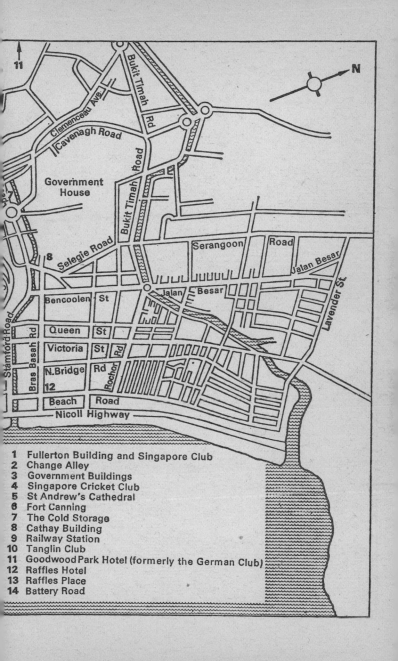

1 Fullerton Building and Singapore Club
2 Change Alley
3 Government Buildings
4 Singapore Cricket Club
5 St Andrew's Cathedral
6 Fort Canning
7 The Cold Storage
8 Cathay Building
9 Railway Station
10 Tanglin Club
11 Goodwood Park Hotel (formerly the German Club)
12 Raffles Hotel
13 Raffles Place
14 Battery Road

Author's Note

Much of this book has been the result of conversations with the many friends I have in Singapore, where I lived in 1938–9 as editor of a daily newspaper. I fell in love with Singapore – the city, the island, its people – and my first love has never palled, so that I have been back again and again, watching the changes from the days of the British Raj to the days of independence.

Sometimes it seems impossible to me that I have known T. W. Ong, now one of my closest friends, since the day in 1938 when I landed in Singapore – and landed a job. On the same day I met George Hammonds who, alas, died recently. It is the same with many other friends whose names appear in this book – men and women like 'Buck' and Lucy Buckeridge, Lee Kuan Yew, the Prime Minister, David Marshall, the first Chief Minister.

Not only would I like to thank them all, and many others too numerous to mention, but I would also make the point that because of these friends this book is perhaps a more personal history than is usual.

There is one other point. The details of Britain's defeat in Singapore have been told so often that some might consider a brief résumé sufficient in this story. I feel, however, that the Japanese victory had a profound effect not only on the prestige of the white man throughout Asia, but on the demise of the British Empire, as it was then called. It is intriguing to illustrate the fundamental differences in attitude of 'ordinary' civilians, most of whom were dismayed by the war, and their leaders who had told them that defeat was impossible.

The point has had to be made, not only because of the slurs wrongly cast on 'whisky-swilling planters', but more importantly because of the changing roles of government officials on the one hand, and civilians – the planters, miners, businessmen and so on – on the other. After Raffles established Singapore the officials administered the island while the businessmen made the money, secure in the knowledge that they could safely leave government to officials and the soldiery. But after the First World War, the umbrella of protection afforded by government changed. It was no longer waterproof. The quality of administrators declined.

Without realising what was happening, the planters and businessmen of the Far East were permitting their destinies to be left in the hands of inferior officials – military and political – whose incompetence would never have been tolerated by Raffles. That is why I have dealt with the defeat in Singapore at some length.

Finally, though I cannot thank individually everyone who has helped me, I would particularly like to thank Anthony Davis for his painstaking work in research, and Christopher Warwick for his patience in preparing the first two drafts and then the final manuscript.

NB
London, February 1978

Part One

The Unknown Island
(1819-1941)

1. The Man Behind the Dream

In a world where it is becoming increasingly fashionable for newly independent countries to erase the names of past father figures from their newly printed history books, to topple their statues, to speak of them only with contumely, it is refreshing to find the name of one white man, long since dead, still regarded with respect by the independent country he founded. The man is Sir Thomas Stamford Raffles, the country is the small, prosperous, idyllic island-state of Singapore.

It is all too easy in the first flush of freedom to flush at the same time the hated past down the drain; but that hate is frequently engineered by opportunists seeking power, so that men who toiled to make the desert bloom or to tame the jungle for others of a different race, creed or colour to inherit are reviled, their rapacity magnified, their honest endeavours minimised.

Empires are out of date (and a good thing too, they are a very expensive luxury) but Raffles and Singapore provide a happy exception in a world where denigration would be more usual. The British are proud of his memory because he was not in the accepted sense an empire-builder (though from time to time he did do a bit of snatching); the Singaporeans admire him for having had the perspicacity to start their little country on the right road, and it is one that fundamentally they have kept to throughout their history.

States, islands, cities, towns, villages even, do not grow and prosper unaided. They need the stimulus that only man can provide, a vision that will last, something bestowed to posterity, something of the mind, more precious than the passing moments of either pain or gain. Proverbs in the Bible summed up perfectly the fact that 'Where there is no vision, the people perish'. If the man is bad, the country founders. It was the luck of Singapore (and not only of the British Empire) that such a remarkable man was first on the scene to shape its future by laying foundation stones that have long outlasted its first masters.

All the merits one can think of have been bestowed on Raffles in countless biographies. He was far-sighted, honest, a prodigious worker, he succeeded in spite of the dolts for whom he worked. All of these attributes are true, but one other reason for his success is often omitted from this catalogue, perhaps because it is negative and at first sight might even seem like a handicap. But if one remembers that Raffles's greatest success lay not in founding Singapore, but in determining the way its future should be shaped, how the descendants of its native population should live, then his greatest asset was his lack of single-mindedness; he was master of so many pursuits that, from the very first discussions when he landed on Singapore, the people greeted him as a friend, above suspicion; they were delighted (and astonished) to hear him speak their language fluently, astounded that he knew their manners and customs. He had learned them not because he had to, but because he was fascinated by them.

Raffles was that rare individual, a man who succeeded in several careers at the same time. He was an historian whose contribution to knowledge was rewarded with a knighthood. He was a splendid cartographer, and above all a naturalist of distinction. He was passionately fascinated by the people he met in remote countries, and his love for them made them love him. All this he did while working as a salaried employee of the East India Company.

He was born on 6 July 1781, at sea. His father, Captain Benjamin Raffles, was master of a 260-ton West Indiaman, *Ann*, which was at the time barely twenty-four hours out of Jamaica. When he was twelve Raffles was sent as a boarder to a school in Hammersmith, London, but his father was unable to meet the fees, and at fourtere he became a clerk with the East India Company in Leaden-hall Street.

Two years after Raffles began work, his father died and Raffles's £70-a-year salary became the principal support for his mother and five sisters, to whom he was devoted. To improve his position, Raffles studied languages and science for eight hours each evening. At the office he worked so hard that inevitably he was rewarded with promotion. It came in 1805, when 'John Company' (as the East India Company was often called), concerned about protecting its ships on the China trade route, declared Malacca a Presidency and chose Raffles from among the clerks at East India House to be Assistant Chief Secretary in Penang.

It is typical of Raffles that he occupied the voyage out by learning Malay, so that by the time he reached Penang he could translate and reply to letters from Malayan notables.

He spent two years as Assistant Secretary in Penang, working prodigiously yet also finding time to start his first collection of botanical specimens, before he was ap-pointed Chief Secretary to the Governor of Penang – at £2000 a year. Then in 1809, the Governor-General of India, Lord Minto, who had already been impressed with several of Raffles's highly intelligent reports on ways of safeguarding Britain's Far Eastern trade, asked Raffles to come and discuss the Java question with him.

The island of Java, for long the pride of Holland's Far Eastern territories, had been handed over to Britain for 'safe keeping' when Napoleon annexed Holland in 1810, on the understanding that the island would be returned to Holland after Napoleon was beaten. The Prince of Orange had agreed to this arrangement. The authorities in Java had not. Minto decided that he could not have the French men o' war using Dutch ports at will, for this was three years before Waterloo, and Napoleon was on the rampage. Consequently the occupation of Java was neces-sary, said Minto, 'as a precautionary measure'.

His meeting with Minto was a turning point in Raffles's

career, for the two men's thoughts and plans ran along
similar channels, and when Raffles left Minto in Calcutta,
it was with a handsome promotion. Minto appointed him
Governor-General's agent in Malaya, reporting directly
to him from a new office in Malacca. Indeed, Minto hinted
at a greater prize. If the 'liberation' of Java were successful,
Raffles might well be left there in charge.

The invasion – or liberation, it is a moot point – was
mounted in June 1811. More than 100 British ships and
11,000 men took part in the operation; Raffles travelled
with Minto on the flagship, the *Modeste*, commanded by
Minto's son. It took six weeks for the sailing ships to reach
the coast of Java, where they landed unopposed at a small
village near Batavia. Within four days the capital was in
British hands, and though skirmishes continued in remote
parts of the island, Minto was able to declare complete
victory by September – and announce that the new Lieutenant-Governor would be Stamford Raffles, at a salary of
£8000 a year.

Two vital points emerge as a result of Raffles's term of
office in Java which are relevant to Singapore.

Firstly, he learned so much about the Dutch methods
of colonisation that he never subsequently lost his determination to safeguard Britain's trading posts and sea lanes
against rivals he considered (from first-hand experience)
to be born marauders. Had he not felt so strongly about
the dangers of Dutch encroachment, he might never have
felt so strongly about the need to settle in Singapore.

Secondly, high office with its first taste of real power gave
him an added status. He learned one lesson: there are
moments when it is expedient to take drastic action without necessarily telling your superiors. He did so in Java
(and outrode subsequent criticism). This knowledge enabled him to risk all in Singapore, knowing full well that
the directors of John Company would be furious at the
actions he had taken without express orders from head
office.

He had to be *right*, of course, in the actions he took, but Raffles never suffered from modesty. Perhaps aided by his local knowledge, it apparently never entered his head that he might make a false move; nor did he ever worry about the wrath of those back home in England.

In many ways, Raffles *did* liberate Java – not in the military sense, but in his attitude to the people whom he studied with the greatest care (while also making notes for a history of the island). He certainly made life more worthwhile for the downtrodden peasants; he also did away with scores of archaic laws that dealt not only with major problems such as crop-growing and export dues, but with absurd pettifogging rules that governed the lives and deaths of every man or woman associated, even indirectly, with the Dutch East India Company. He found, for example, that only a senior merchant was permitted to wear a velvet coat; that only the widow of a senior merchant could wear embroidery on her dress at his funeral. Everything – from the number of horses, the type of carriage, even the size of a slave's earrings – was predetermined according to rank. Raffles impatiently brushed these cobwebs aside and made life much easier.

More than anything else, however, Raffles tried to ease the terrible burden of the slaves. A good friend of William Wilberforce, Raffles was horrified when he learned that in Batavia alone there were more than 12,000 slaves – including 165 who belonged to one rich householder. Raffles was unable to stamp out slavery in Java, but he was successful in outlawing slave *trading*. By banning the trade he attacked the root of the problem, for the dealers – the equivalent of today's drug pushers – did everything to encourage slavery.

Raffles ruled Java until March 1816, revolutionising the Dutch colonial system under which Javanese peasants had been told what to grow and were paid whatever the Dutch thought fit. Raffles allowed them to grow what they wished and to sell in an open market at prevailing prices. But though enlightened, it was inevitably less profitable, and Java failed to pay its way. The head office in London became critical. There were also steps afoot to return Java to Holland.

Raffles left Java after being promised the post of Lieutenant-Governor of Bencoolen, the British outpost in Sumatra. He was deeply hurt at being ordered out of Java before it was restored to Holland. In fact the step was taken because of certain charges that were being made against him – including one that he had dishonestly made money out of land speculation. Unknown to him, John Company was seeking to depose his authority and behind his back had written to the Governor-General of Bengal, 'Whatever may be the result of the charges preferred against Mr Raffles, we are of the opinion that his continuance in the Government of Java would be highly inexpedient.'

Even though Raffles was completely exonerated from the allegations of dishonesty, it took the East India Company directors more than six months to clear his name. It is typical of Raffles that he did not bother to await the verdict before embarking on other ventures, as though he were so convinced of his innocence that he shrugged the matter off. For it was at this time that – back in London – two great events helped him to shape his life – he married for the second time, and he published his famous work, *History of Java*.

Even before its publication in May 1817, Raffles was being lionised. 'The Java question' – to keep or return the island – was the news of the day and Raffles was in the centre of it. And, too, London 'society' was astounded by his other work. He had been elected a Fellow of the Royal Society; was already suggesting the formation of the London Zoo. The public announcement by John Company of his innocence was front-page news. So when he dedicated *Java* to the Prince Regent, the Prince invited him to Carlton House and when Raffles arrived, asked everyone to be silent while he delivered a twenty-minute eulogy of the author. After that, he asked him to kneel.

And after *that*, the Prince said, 'Arise, Sir Stamford Raffles.'

Sir Stamford and Lady Raffles sailed from Falmouth for Bencoolen in October 1817 on a new company ship, the *Lady Raffles*. Bencoolen – a slice of land on the coast of the island of Sumatra – had been in British hands since 1685, but though Raffles's appointment as Lieutenant-Governor must have been something of a let-down after his term of office in Java, the truth is that there was at the time no other important post available. Waterloo had been won and the Dutch were taking back their colonies. Britain had been too busy fighting a war to expand her empire. In fact Raffles, now thirty-six, was lucky to find the Bencoolen post vacant at just the right time, though he wrote to his friend William Marsden, 'This is without exception the most wretched place I have ever beheld.'

Even so, it was during the years in Bencoolen that Raffles was able to devote more time to his studies of zoology, natural history and, more important from history's point of view, to the need for another trading station, for in fact he was more than a mere Lieutenant-Governor. He was a spy. His warnings against Dutch aggrandisement had been heeded in London where it had been made clear to him before sailing that London expected to receive 'early and constant information' about the plans of Dutch and other nations in the area, and Raffles was specifically asked to send details, together with 'such observations as may occur to you whether of a political or commercial nature' as urgently as possible, and if necessary in secret.

The orders suited Raffles, who was now in a position to back up the warnings he had put on paper in London. The Dutch were trying to restrict British trade, he said, by a 'system of taking possession of unoccupied ports and making treaties of monopoly with the natives'. Britain should adopt the same tactics before it was too late. In one despatch from Bencoolen he wrote:

The Dutch possess the only passes through which ships must sail into this archipelago, the Straits of Sunda and of Malacca; and the British have not now an inch of ground to stand upon between the Cape of Good Hope and China, nor a single friendly port at which they can water or obtain refreshments ... it is indispensable that some regular and accredited authority on the part of the British Government should exist in the archipelago.

Fortunately the Marquis of Hastings, at the time Governor-General of Bengal, was so impressed with the arguments that he sent for Raffles, who arrived in Calcutta within three months (a short time in those days) to find Hastings equally determined that Britain should establish a trading port near the Straits of Malacca which dominated the trade route to China.

To Raffles, one spot stood out: Rhio. But no one was certain whether it was in Dutch hands or not, so Hastings, when authorising Raffles to explore possibilities in the area, suggested that it might be a good idea to visit Johore. What is really astonishing when writing of such a leisurely age – where it took up to six months for a letter from Penang to reach England – is to find a sudden burst of speed quite unsuited to the times. One thinks that Raffles, after talking with Hastings, might have returned to Bencoolen, pondered events, perhaps written to London, discussed plans, and finally – but when? – taken action.

Not at all. The zest and verve which he now displayed outshone even his remarkable speed in writing *Java*. In the autumn of 1818 he was still in Calcutta. Yet before the end of the year Raffles had travelled to Penang, from where he had sent out a colleague, Major Farquhar, to spy out the prospects (particularly Rhio) after which, in secret, he finalised arrangements for a small fleet to sail south in early January.

It was a remarkable feat – helped, of course, by the fact that Raffles did not bother to inform London of his detailed plans; and also because he knew that every day counted; for once the Dutch heard of any British plans, they would be able from their nearby bases to forestall them.

So in mid-January 1819, Raffles sailed south. What is more, he knew just where he was going. He had already written to Marsden, 'We are now on the way to the eastward, in the hope of doing something ... and you must not be surprised if my next letter to you is dated from the site of the ancient city of Singapura.'

2. The City of the Lion

The *Indiana*, which had taken nine days to make her way southwards from Penang, rounded the point shortly after noon on 27 January 1819 and sailed due east. She was barely ninety miles north of the equator, and the heat was intolerable, while the harsh sun dancing on the water blinded the eyes, until in the late afternoon a touch of cool breeze sprang up and the temperature dropped a couple of degrees.

Raffles was on the bridge, incongruously dressed in stout broadcloth, his neck imprisoned in a cravat, his legs in thick stockings. By now, though only thirty-seven, scholarship and the tropics had between them marked him with a stoop and slightly hollow cheeks. But he was still a handsome man, just under six feet tall, with a broad brow topped by fair hair, a large, generous mouth beneath a high nose.

He waited until the *Indiana* was abreast of the low, marshy swampland of the island, with the jungle meeting the sky in the background, and signalled to the captain, James Pearl. The anchor chains clanged down. The *Indiana*'s escorting vessels – two frigates and three small merchantmen – hove to. Through his telescope, Raffles could make out a cluster of attap huts near the shore, and one building that was conspicuously more imposing than the others. And that, he knew, meant the presence of a local ruler, probably a Malay prince, with the title of Temenggong.

This was his first sight of Singapore, and though Raffles was always more concerned with future possibilities than present appearances, we know what the island looked like from a report made by Captain Ross, one of John Company's marine experts, who, when writing about it, elevated Singapore to the status of 'town':

> The town of Singapura, on the island of the same name, stands on a point of land near the western part of a bay, and is easily distinguished by there being just behind it a pleasant-looking hill that is partly cleared of trees, and between the point on which the town is situated and the western end of the bay there is a creek in which the native vessels anchor close to the town, so it may be found useful to European vessels of easy draft to refill in. On the eastern side of the bay, opposite to the town, there is a deep inlet lined by mangroves, which would also be a good anchorage for native boats; and about north from the low sandy point of the bay there is a village inhabited by fishermen, and a short way to the eastward there is a passage through the mangroves leading to a fresh-water river.

Almost before anchors had rattled down, a few natives were paddling towards the *Indiana*. They were obviously friendly, and crew members helped them aboard, and Raffles, in his impeccable Malay, asked one of them to convey to the Temenggong the message that he would be honoured if he could land and call on him the following day.

It was 4 pm on 28 January 1819. Ten days later, the Union Jack was flying over the scrub and swamp, labourers were building a fort and houses, and the free port of Singapore had been founded.

*

At the time, Singapura was marked on only a few local charts, but because of his knowledge of Malay history, geography and customs, Raffles was aware of its position. His first choice had been to establish a port on Rhio, twenty miles to the south; only when he realised that the Dutch were already there did he consider landing at Singapore. Even so, his knowledge enabled him to realise its potential before seeing it. Two weeks before sailing, he had written to Bengal:

The island of Sincapore [sic], independently of the straits and harbour of Johore, which it both forms and commands, has, on its southern shores, and by means of the several smaller islands which lie off it, excellent anchorage and smaller harbours, and seems in every respect most peculiarly adapted for our object. Its position in the straits of Singapore is far more convenient and commanding than even Rhio, for our China trade passing down the straits of Malacca, and every native vessel that sails through the Straits of Rhio must pass in sight of it.

The town of Johore is, in the main, at some distance up the river, the banks of which are said to be low; but, on the score of salubrity, there does not seem to be any objection to a station at Sincapore, or on the opposite shore towards Point Romanea, or on any of the smaller islands which lie off this part of the coast. The larger harbour of Johore is declared by professional men whom I have consulted, and by every Eastern trader of experience to whom I have been able to refer, to be capacious and easily defensible and, the British flag once hoisted, there would be no want of supplies to meet the immediate necessities of our establishment.

No wonder that his first anxious question to the islanders who paddled out to greet him was, 'Where are the nearest Dutchmen?' With relief he learned there were none nearer than Rhio.

Next morning, Raffles was paddled to the shore by

canoe. Major William Farquhar of the Madras Engineers, who was in charge of the military contingent on the frigates, accompanied him. Raffles, who detested any display of force, insisted, despite Farquhar's grumbles, that only one sepoy, armed with a musket, should accompany them. Every action must emphasise that this was a friendly mission, not an expedition of conquest.

Raffles – first and foremost the natural historian – looked around as they glided up the curling Singapore River, which ran much the same course as it does today which emitted the same smells, compounded of dried fish and spices, an odour distinctive to Singapore, and which, even today, every Singaporean recognises when he returns home. It was not an unpleasant smell, but once smelt, it was never forgotten. The sluggish waterway was choked with mangrove swamp. Raffles had to help force a passage through the evil-looking trees, with their roots trailing down from the trunk above the water into the sludge below, forming props for the trees yet looking strangely dead and sinister.

About forty yards up river, Raffles signalled for the canoe to stop. The mangroves had thinned out. To the left he could see swamp studded with a few coconut trees in that section of the island where Raffles Place stands today. On his right the ground was more solid, and he could make out a village of sorts – forty or fifty mat huts dominated by the larger house of the local ruler, whose name was Abdul Rahman. This presumably was Captain Ross's 'town'.

In the early nineteenth century, ceremony counted more than it does today, perhaps even more so in remote settlements, so despite the heat Raffles was dressed in much the same formal dress he might have worn for a meeting in rainy London. His dark coat (coloured coats had gone out of fashion) had long tails, and his waistcoat was adorned with gold seals on a heavy watch chain. His trousers were cut tight at the knee and tucked into high boots. His shirt was ruffled, with a high collar and stock at his throat. To complete the outfit he wore a curly-brimmed beaver hat.

Farquhar was sweating in his thick uniform. Both men must have envied the more comfortable sarong of the Temenggong who strode forward to greet them.

It is curious to reflect how little man changes in his approach to strangers when business affairs are to be transacted. The Jim Slaters of today, anxious to clinch a deal over lunch at Goodwood Park, would never dream of discussing the only matter that interested them until the coffee had been served, and it was the same in the days of Raffles. Relays of Malays in sarongs offered the visitors local fruits – tiny, sweet speckled bananas, rambutans, starfruit – in baskets of platted banana leaves, but any attempt to discuss business – and after all, Raffles was planning quite a take-over bid – before the tropical repast was ended would have been an affront to the dignity of Abdul Rahman. One can imagine Raffles and Farquhar, sitting on makeshift stools, their thick clothes drenched in sweat, smiling politely, Raffles making small talk, while wondering whether they dared to refuse any more food.

Finally, the tedious business of eating was over and Raffles came to the point. The British wished to settle and trade in Singapore. They would of course pay a handsome rent and obviously the islanders would benefit as well as the British.

There was, however, a serious snag. As the Temenggong explained, the island belonged to Johore, separated from the north shores of the island by a narrow strip of water, and the consent of the Sultan would be necessary. Normally this might have presented no difficulty, but the problem was compounded by the fact that Johore was in the midst of a constitutional problem.

The succession to the Sultancy was in dispute. Sultan Mohamed had died six years previously. The eldest of his sons, Hussein, generally known as Tengku Long, was absent from Johore when his father died, and when he returned, his brother Muda, who had been acting as Regent, refused to relinquish power, and had been recognised by the Dutch (as good neighbours) as the rightful Sultan.

Raffles immediately realised three things: firstly, the

Dutch would veto any attempt to deal with Muda; secondly, Muda, who obviously had no rightful claim to rule Johore, was a puppet of the Dutch. So, as Raffles argued, if he could persuade the rightful ruler, Tengku Long, to return with British backing (and British protection) he might easily agree to allow Britain to establish a 'factory'. (The word 'factory', used to describe every British trading post, was a relic of the early Portuguese adventurers who established a *feitoria* in each area where their merchants settled.)

Tengku Long was nursing his grievances in the nearby island of Bulang. Raffles sent two Malays to ask him to come to Singapore, and seemed confident of the outcome, for he persuaded Abdul Rahman to allow him to disembark three hundred sepoys and one hundred sailors to start operations. The Malay prince, it seems, was delighted – not only by Raffles's charm, but also because he could not believe that any white man could speak such perfect Malay, with such a command of nuance and idiom.

Not only that. As well as being aware of the island's size (it covers 224 square miles and is almost exactly the same size and diamond shape as the Isle of Wight, measuring 26 miles across, 14 miles from north to south), Raffles was soon drawing on his profound knowledge of its history and giving Abdul Rahman a lesson, going back to the days when the Malays named it Temasek, from *tasek*, meaning the sea.

Six centuries before Raffles arrived, it had been a flourishing city – 'the Constantinople of the Eastern seas', as one writer put it. It was a seat of learning, a busy commercial centre, founded in 1160, according to local legend, by a Malayan prince from Palembang, the Sumatran capital of the Hindu–Buddhist empire of Sry Vijaya. He saw an animal with 'a head jet black, its breast white, its size rather larger than a he-goat'. He thought it was a lion, though probably it was a tiger, so named the island Singapura, from the Sanskrit *singa* for 'lion' and *pura* for 'city'.

The city flourished for two hundred years until it was

conquered by a Javanese ruler, the Rajah of Majapahit. The few survivors fled, Singapura declined in importance, and by the time Raffles arrived, it had reverted to a small fishing village and the haunt of pirates.

Raffles was by no means the first Britisher to set foot on Singapore – though he was the first to see its possibilities. One man actually refused the island when it was offered to him as a gift. Alexander Hamilton, a Scot, called at Johore in 1703 on his way to China and, so he claimed, was offered Singapore as a present by the king. Captain Hamilton wrote, 'I told him it could be of no use to a private person.' That was more than a century before Raffles arrived to find Singapore inhabited by perhaps 120 Malays, a few dozen Chinese, some independent fishermen and, from time to time, pirates.

The next morning the sepoys landed, cleared a patch of scrub and pitched tents. They dug a well. A cannon was brought ashore and Raffles ordered it to be mounted at the top of a 150-foot hill near the beach – a suggestion causing alarm among the islanders, as this was Bukit Larangan, the Forbidden Hill, where the ancient kings had lived and were buried. Raffles observed crisply that it was probably healthier at the top than at sea level and tramped up the overgrown path to the top of the rise, from which he could see the dozens of small islands dotting the shimmering sea, the possibilities of a great harbour, and behind him the forest and jungle. He gave orders for the path to be opened, and a cannon was dragged to the summit of Fort Canning, as it was later called.

Within the week on 5 February – Tengku Long arrived in Singapore, having left his island on the pretext of going fishing. He was hardly the type of man to appeal to the fastidious Raffles, for he was grossly fat, and spoke in a toneless voice; he was terrified of Raffles's intentions, and was at first convinced that he had been sent for only to be arrested. He was the more intrigued because Raffles was nowhere to be seen when he arrived. The Englishman had remained on board, and only came ashore after seeing

Tengku Long arrive.

The Tengku was soon put at ease. According to one of Raffles's helpers, Munshi Abdullah.

> Mr Raffles showed Tengku Long every honour and re-
> spect and brought him to a place where they all sat
> down on chairs. [Raffles] kept bowing his head and was
> as sweet as a sea of honey. Not merely the human heart
> but even a stone would be broken by hearing such words
> as his with a gentle voice like the sweetest music.

Abdullah, who had a poetic nature and at times enjoyed poetic licence, added, 'The sincerity of Mr Raffles became evident to Tengku Long. In a moment his sadness changed to gladness and his face lighted up.' In fact, Tengku Long finally became so enthusiastic that he proposed massacring the Dutch on Rhio, an idea which Raffles had to discourage.

A ceremony was arranged for 6 February. The ships were dressed overall. The thirty Europeans wore full uniform and the troops were drawn up on parade. Three chairs were set out in a tent, one for Raffles, one for Farquhar and the other for the new Sultan. A light rain fell, which the Malays interpreted as a sign of blessings to come.

Even in those days Raffles knew the value of the red-carpet treatment, and at 1 pm he formally received the new Sultan, who walked the strip of red carpet brought from the ship. Two lines of sepoys presented arms as he sat on his makeshift throne. The Malays crowded the beach, their leaders holding the sacred yellow umbrella. The Tengku was sweating profusely; every Briton doffed his hat as a mark of respect to the ruler, while a proclamation was read out that Tengku Long had been appointed Sultan Hussein 'in the town of Singapore and in the districts and shores thereof' by the authority of the Governor-General of Bengal. Raffles had not, of course, had any opportunity to apprise the Governor-General of his action, but that was not the kind of trifle to worry him.

Then Raffles read the treaty he had written on thick foolscap – in English on the left, in Malay on the right. In return for the right granted to the East India Company to maintain a settlement at Singapore, the Sultan was to receive $5,000 a year and the Temenggong $3,000 a year. (Spanish dollars were then universal currency in the archipelago.) The British would carry out and pay for administration and provide protection, while the Sultan agreed not to let any other nation occupy or trade on the island, resisting any invaders by force if necessary. British jurisdiction extended from Tanjong (Cape) Mallang in the west to Tanjong Katong in the east, and as far inland 'as the range of cannon shot'.

The East India Company seal was impressed in red wax and the Sultan's with lamp-black. Presents were distributed; Raffles gave the Sultan lengths of black and yellow cloth and $1,000 on account. The Union Jack was hoisted on a 36-foot-high flagstaff that had been set in the sand, and salutes were fired by the guns of the frigates and the shore battery. Drinks were served, toasts drunk, and the ceremony ended at 4 pm.

Raffles now issued a proclamation appointing Major Farquhar as Resident and commander of the troops in Singapore. 'All persons are hereby directed to obey Major Farquhar accordingly,' it ended. Farquhar's appointment was only temporary – at the specific request of the major, who was due to go on leave and only agreed to stay at Raffles's urgent request. Because Farquhar insisted on being released as soon as possible by a permanent Resident, he was given handsome temporary allowances – a generous gesture with unfortunate consequences.

So ended one of the greatest days in the life of Raffles, who later wrote in a letter:

Here I am in Singapore ... and in the enjoyment of all the pleasures which a footing on such classic ground may inspire. The British Union Jack waves unmolested. Most certainly the Dutch never had a factory in the island of Singapore and it does not appear to me that their recent arrangements at Rhio can, or ought to, interfere with our permanent establishment here. This place possesses an excellent harbour and ... we have commanded an intercourse with all the ships passing through the Straits of Singapore. We are within a week's sail of China, close to Siam and in the very seat of the Malayan empire.

To the Duchess of Somerset, with whom Raffles maintained a correspondence for many years, he wrote 'directions' for finding his new treasure:

Follow me from Calcutta, within the Nicobar and Andaman Islands, to the Prince of Wales's Island, then accompany me down the Straits of Malacca, past the town of Malacca, and round the southwestern point of the Peninsula. You will then enter what are called the Straits of Singapore, and in Marsden's map of Sumatra you will observe an island to the north of these straits called Singapura; this is the spot, the site of the ancient maritime capital of the Malays, and within the walls of these fortifications, raised not less than six centuries ago, on which I have planted the British flag, where, I trust, it will long triumphantly wave.

To his old friend William Marsden, he summed up, in a few lines, his philosophy of Singapore: 'If I keep Singapore I shall be quite satisfied; and in a few years our influence over the Archipelago, as far as concerns our commerce, will be fully established.'

Raffles knew that the Dutch would be furious, but as he wrote in another letter:

We may, I think, combat their arguments without any difficulty. They had established themselves at Rhio and by virtue of a treaty which they had forced the Raja of that place to sign, they assume the right of excluding us from all the islands and declaring the people their vassals. The legitimate successor to the empire of Johore is with us and on the ruins of the ancient capital has signed a treaty with us.

Raffles had an essentially pragmatic approach to every basic problem – he was the sort of man who knew just what he wanted – so though he did not intend to remain for long, he moved ashore next day to an attap hut built at the end of Singapore Point, and gave Farquhar detailed instructions about the establishment of Singapore as a free port, charging no customs dues. Farquhar started to build himself a house where the Cricket Club now stands. The first harbour-master was to be Raffles's brother-in-law, Captain Flint, married to Raffles's sister Mary.

He also arranged plans for the defence of the island. Sepoys started to build a fort big enough to house ten guns and thirty European artillery men – and the rest of the garrison in an emergency. But he emphasised that Farquhar must never interfere with the Dutch where they had authority, nor provoke them. He appointed a lieutenant of the Bengal Artillery as Farquhar's assistant.

Before embarking, Raffles made a tour of the island. At the mouth of the river he saw a large, flat stone surrounded by hundreds of human skulls. When he was told that many were the heads of pirate victims or of pirates killed in fights, Raffles had them all gathered in sacks which were weighted with stones and buried at sea. Then he embarked for Penang to file his official report to the Supreme Government:

Situated at the extremity of the peninsula, all vessels to and from China via Malacca are obliged to pass within five miles of our headquarters, and generally pass within half a mile of St John's, a dependent islet forming the western point of the bay, in which I have directed a small post to be fixed, and from whence every ship can be boarded if necessary, the water being smooth at all seasons. The run between these islands and the Karimuns, which are within sight from it, can be effected in a few hours, and crosses the route which all vessels from the Netherlands must necessarily pursue when bound towards Batavia and the Eastern islands.

He went into great detail about the practicalities involved in setting up a new station. The port would, he
explained, be used by ships for 'refreshment'. There were
sufficient Chinese already living in Singapore to supply
vegetables and other provisions for ships. There was a
plentiful supply of fish and turtles, while 'rice, salt and
other necessaries are always procurable from Siam, the
granary of the Malay tribes in this quarter'.

But always – again and again, as though to forestall
criticism – he reiterated its value as a base, not only for
the present, but in the future, as a duty-free post:

> By maintaining our right to a free commerce with the
> Malay States and inspiring them with a confidence in
> the stability of it, we may contemplate its advancement
> to a much greater extent than has hitherto been enjoyed.
> Independently of our commerce with the tribes of the
> archipelago, Singapore may be considered as the princi-
> pal entrepot to which the native traders of Siam, Cam-
> bodia, Champa, Cochin China, and China the same time
> of one of the least troublesome and expensive, which
> we possess. Our object is not territory, but trade; a
> great commercial emporium ... One free port in these
> seas must eventually destroy the spell of Dutch mono-
> poly, and what Malta is in the West, that may Singapore
> be in the East.

He was well satisfied with what he had accomplished,
but knew there would be repercussions as soon as the
Dutch discovered what he had done, and was far from
certain that London would endorse all he had achieved.

He was right to be apprehensive, but Raffles had weath-
ered complaints about his conduct before.

3. 'A Child of my Own'

For the next four months Britain was under severe pressure to hand Singapore over to the Dutch who were furious at what they considered trickery on the part of Raffles. The Governor-General of Java, Baron van der Capellan, claimed that Raffles had seized a part of the Dutch empire, that a Dutch treaty with the Sultan of Johore in 1795 had placed Singapore under the control of Malacca. This meant, he argued, that Singapore was a Dutch dependency. Timmerman Thyssen, the opium-growing Dutch governor in Malacca, was so incensed that he threatened to sail to Singapore and drag Farquhar away in chains.

This was bad enough, but the Dutch had also exerted pressure on the fat, ineffectual Tengku Long and the Temenggong, who lost their nerve and were prevailed upon to write whimpering letters to the Dutch saying that Raffles had obtained their agreement by force and threats. Raffles, who had returned to Bencoolen, does not appear to have taken these local setbacks very seriously at first, but when the Dutch started waving the letters as 'proof' that Britain had occupied Singapore by force, they found an unexpected ally in the pompous British Governor of Penang (or Prince of Wales Island as it was then called). Colonel Bannerman had long nursed a jealousy of the success enjoyed by Raffles, and was also probably concerned lest a thriving Singapore diminish the influence of his own domain.

Almost at the same time as the Dutch in Malacca sent their protest to Penang (accompanied by copies of the two spurious letters) Bannerman also received an urgent request from Farquhar in Singapore for military reinforcements and cash. Farquhar was not afraid, but he wanted to show the flag to stiffen any wavering fears among the local population, since the Dutch were threatening a resort to arms unless Farquhar left the island.

It was, of course, an idle threat. Holland had been stripped bare by Napoleon and could hardly have mustered an honour guard in the area, let alone the vessels required to mount an invasion. But Bannerman, suffering perhaps from pique, elected to take the threat seriously and sent an abject apology to Timmerman Thyssen, begging him to avoid war, adding, 'I am the more induced to make this appeal to you as Sir Stamford Raffles is not under the control of this government.' (As Raffles was Lieutenant-Governor at Bencoolen, 'this government' no doubt referred to Penang.)

Bannerman also refused flatly to send any men or money to Singapore – the occupation of which, he pointed out acidly, he had opposed from the first. Then he wrote a long letter to Lord Hastings in Calcutta. The screed of many pages was peppered with sententious nonsense. He had refused to send troops, he said, because 'It must be notorious that any force we are able to despatch to Singapore could not resist the overpowering armament at the disposal of the Batavia government.' But then he went too far, by inferring that 'Sir Stamford Raffles has occupied that island in violation of the orders of the Supreme Government.'

Nothing emphasises the stupidity of Bannerman more than this sentence, for Hastings was the one man who had encouraged Raffles in the venture; consequently any attack on Raffles was a direct reflection on the wisdom of Hastings. Furiously, he sent Bannerman a frosty rebuke, telling him that he was 'entirely wrong in determining so broadly against the propriety of the step taken by Sir Thomas Raffles'. Within three days of receiving the letter, Bannerman sent 200 troops and $6000 to Farquhar.

Farquhar meanwhile had confronted the Sultan and Temenggong and obtained from each a retraction of their letters saying the British had used force, each one reaffirming in florid (and identical) language, 'I here call

God and His Prophet to witness that the English established themselves at Singapore with my free will and
consent, and that from the arrival of the Honourable Sir
Thomas Stamford Raffles no troops or effects were landed,
or anything executed, but with the free accord of myself
and of the Sultan of Johore.'

Time was on Raffles's side. It took days for the despatch
prows to carry letters between Batavia, Malacca, Rhio,
Singapore and Penang, let alone Calcutta, and each passing day made the British presence in Singapore safer,
particularly when the news of Raffles's coup appeared in
the *Calcutta Journal* and was not only acclaimed by that
newspaper, but applauded by merchants fearful of Dutch
attempts to establish a trade monopoly. That was enough
for Hastings to write a partial commitment to Raffles: 'It
is intended to maintain the post of Singapore for the
present.'

'For the present' had an ominous ring; it meant that
some politicians still opposed any steps that would an-
tagonise the Dutch, and in today's hurried world the
Dutch might have taken speedy action, but Raffles wrote
placating letters promising to relinquish Singapore if the
Dutch could prove their case; knowing that the time
factor would decide the argument. It was September before
the news of the British settlement in Singapore appeared
in *The Times* in London, which hailed the event with a
flowery leading article (written, in fact, not by *The Times*,
but copied word for word from the *Calcutta Journal*). It
read in part:

We believe and earnestly hope that the establishment of
a settlement under such favourable circumstances, and
at a moment when we had every reason to fear that the
efforts of the Dutch had been successful in excluding us
altogether from the Eastern Archipelago, will receive
all the support which is necessary to its progress, and
that by its rapid advance in wealth, industry and population, which in their establishment and development
from the most honourable monuments of statesmen, it

will attest hereafter the wisdom and foresight of the present administration, and its attention to the commercial and political interests of our country.

We congratulate our Eastern friends, and the commercial world in general, on the event which we this day report to them. They will rejoice in our having occupied the position which was required as a fulcrum for the support of our Eastern and China trade and from whence we can extend our commercial views and speculations. The spell of Dutch monopoly, so justly reviled and detested, and which had nearly been again established, has been dissolved by the ethereal touch of that wand which broke in pieces the confederacy that lately threatened our continental possessions.

Yet it was to be three years before Britain gave official approval to Raffles's initiative. Long before then the Dutch had given up any hope of hauling down the Union Jack.

Raffles returned to Singapore in June 1819, and he could hardly believe his eyes as he viewed the astonishing transformation that had taken place in four months. The population had grown from less than 200 to 5000. The harbour was alive with shipping, and, as he wrote, 'Everyone is comfortably housed, provisions are in abundance, the troops healthy.'

The new inhabitants were mainly Chinese who had moved from Malacca and Rhio. Farquhar had sent news of the British settlement by sampan, inviting men to come and trade. Some fell victim to pirates; forty Malays sailing from Malacca in one boat were murdered. Others were turned back by a Dutch gunboat patrolling the straits. But hundreds did get through, bringing ducks, fruit, vegetables and other provisions with which to begin trading. The incentives were clear. In the past, Chinese traders had resorted to Manila and Brunei, but in both places they had been ill-treated. In Brunei the government had become rapacious and the Chinese no longer dared even approach the coast. In Manila the atmosphere was already unfriendly and in 1820 an epidemic was ascribed to foreigners poisoning the water, which led to a massacre of English, Dutch, French, Americans and more than eighty Chinese. So the Chinese were quick to take up Farquhar's invitation.

Many came from the Dutch settlement of Malacca – making the Dutch more furious. The prospect of trade was far better in Singapore which was expanding while Malaccan trade was shrinking. Quite apart from onerous taxation, the lives of the natives in Malacca were still ordered by the same kind of petty laws so beloved by the Dutch, and which had so irritated Raffles in Java. Very often, fines for infringements of local 'laws' were used to supplement taxes. (One law stipulated that the road in front of each house must *always* be kept scrupulously clean, and one official, nicknamed 'Mr Broom', made it his business to inspect the streets daily; he would wait until a couple of carriages dirtied the street. Then he would pounce.) According to Abdullah, the exodus became so serious that the Dutch rushed through a special promulgation banning anyone in Malacca from 'emigrating' to Singapore. It had little effect in an area where anyone could slip away by land or sea at night.

Farquhar had dealt with one local 'nuisance' – Singapore island was infested by rats, which even crawled over his bed at night; so he offered an anna for each carcass. Some men arrived with as many as sixty, costing so much that he had to reduce the bounty. But the campaign was so effective that he launched a similar one to rid the island of stinging centipedes. (After which, on a riverside walk, he lost his dog to an 18-foot alligator.) There was, however, one terrible problem that Farquhar found impossible to eradicate – one that all but cost him his life, and which still persists to this day. It is the fearful, inexplicable outburst of demented frenzy which causes the people of Malaya to run amok – for no apparent reason to attack, maim, kill anyone near them during a period of frenzy that lends them an almost incredible strength.

Farquhar was the victim of the first recorded case in Singapore of a man running amok. His assailant, named Syden Yassin, had been sued for $1400 by a merchant. When he could not pay, Farquhar, as chief magistrate, committed him to jail. Security was lax and Yassin was not searched; he had a *kris* hidden in his clothes. That evening hé sought permission to visit the merchant and seek time to pay. He was allowed out under guard. As he entered the merchant's garden he drew the *kris*. The merchant fled out of the back door to Farquhar's nearby home. Yassin killed the guard. Armed only with a stick, Farquhar set out to deal with Yassin, but the Arab hurled himself from the darkness and stabbed Farquhar in the chest, though the wound was not serious. At this moment Farquhar's son Andrew and some sepoys arrived. Andrew slashed the Arab's face with a sword and the sepoys bayoneted him to death. When Raffles arrived, believing Farquhar to be dead, troops were bringing up guns to deal with what was thought to be a Malay revolt. Raffles established the facts, stood the troops down and calmed the situation.

Next day he had the body of Yassin paraded around the island in a cart, preceded by a man with a gong, and then hung in an iron cage to deter anyone else from running amok. In this he was unsuccessful.

(No one has explained satisfactorily why the term 'running amok' should be employed only where Malays are concerned. It may be the result of language – the Malays used the word *amok* (pronounced *amo*, with the 'k' mute) for 'sudden savagery', and so probably it became associated with them. One theory was offered by Sir William Norris in 1846, when giving judgement in an amok case in which a Malay in Penang had killed four. Drawing attention to the fact that the murderer was a Moslem he said, 'Not that I wish to brand Mahomedans in general as worse than all other men. I merely state the fact that such atrocities disgrace no other creed.')

Fortunately cases were rare, and did nothing to deter

flocks of settlers from arriving, and even at this early date, it was clear to Raffles that Singapore would soon outstrip both Penang and Malacca in volume of trade. Always pragmatic, he told Farquhar to clear the jungle and lay out roads and sites for houses, allocating separate areas for Chinese, Malays and Indians, with a code of regulations to cover a mixed community. He established a land registry, then planned roads on a grid pattern, with the main roads parallel to the harbour and the secondary roads crossing them at right-angles. People who today walk or ride along the wide, spacious streets of Singapore – surely more handsome than in any other Asian city – may reflect that from the very beginning Raffles gave firm orders regulating the width of all roads and streets, and orders to 'attend to the settlement's beauty, regularity and cleanliness' – instructions that are still obeyed to this day. Raffles also ordered a bridge to be built across the river into the harbour. This was the first Elgin Bridge.

Nearly a thousand labourers worked at jungle-clearing and construction, with the aid of bullocks which Raffles had sent to Singapore. A gardener named Dunn arrived with spice plants which he planted on Government Hill, the former Forbidden Hill. He also planted 125 trees. Raffles sorted out an early muddle, for Farquhar had sold plots of land freehold, which was contrary to company policy. Raffles arranged for the buyers' money to be returned, then sold them 99-year leases.

Singapore, he wrote to a friend, 'is a child of my own. But for my Malay studies I should hardly have known that such a place existed. Not only the European but the Indian world was also ignorant of it.'

Always aware that the future of Singapore rested on its achievements as a free trading post, Raffles never forgot the importance of the merchants on whose abilities and goodwill the port depended, and (unlike many other British officials) went to great lengths to see that they were treated with circumspection and had a voice in the government of the island. In one letter to the Supreme Government, he wrote:

I am satisfied that nothing has tended more to the discomfort and constant jarrings which have hitherto occurred in our remote settlements than the policy which has dictated the exclusion of the European merchants from all share, much less credit, in the domestic regulation of the settlement of which they are frequently its most important members.

At the end of July, well pleased, Raffles and his family sailed for Bencoolen – and on the voyage were given proof of the hatred which the Dutch still nursed against Raffles. Their vessel ran aground on a sandbank in the Straits of Rhio. To lighten ship, the water casks were emptied, and the ship refloated, after which the captain sent a boat ashore to the Dutch settlement on Rhio with a request for water. When the Dutch Resident heard that Raffles was on board he refused any assistance. Luckily a more friendly American clipper came to his help.

At Bencoolen, Raffles waited impatiently for official news from London as to the fate of Singapore, for there was still much criticism of him in England. Lord Bathurst, Secretary of the Colonies, described him in the House of Lords as 'a mere trade agent who had caused embarrassment to the government'. Raffles was wounded by such criticism – especially as reports from Singapore continued to be encouraging. Farquhar, who had been promoted to Lieutenant-Colonel, wrote to Raffles in March 1820:

Nothing can possibly exceed the rising trade and general prosperity of this infant colony. Indeed, to look at our harbour just now, where upwards of twenty junks, three of which are from China, two from Cochin China and the rest from Siam and other quarters are at anchor, beside ships, brigs, prows etc., a person would naturally exclaim: 'Surely this cannot be an establishment of only twelve months' standing.'

Then a series of personal tragedies overwhelmed Raffles. Three of his four children, whom he adored, died. His eldest son Leopold died of suspected cholera in 1821. The following year a second son and a daughter died within ten days of each other after contracting dysentery. Only Ella, the youngest, survived, and Raffles sent her back to England in the care of the nurse, Mrs Grimes. 'My heart is sick and nigh broken,' he declared. His own health, which had long been fragile, worsened.

Nevertheless, in September 1822 he made his third, his longest, and what was to be his last visit to Singapore. It had a tonic effect upon him. 'The coldest and most disinterested could not land in Singapore without surprise and emotion,' he wrote. 'I already feel differently. I feel a new life and vigour about me and if it please God to grant me health, the next six months will, I hope, make some amends for the gloom of the last sixteen. Rob me not of this, my political child, and you may yet see me home in all my wonted spirits.' He moved into a newly built, wooden-walled bungalow, completed in two weeks, on Government Hill. Outside the bungalow he started to lay out an experimental garden.

It was three years since he had last seen Singapore and the insignificant fishing village had grown into a bustling boom town of nearly ten thousand. Farquhar showed him the figures behind its prosperity. In the first two and a half years 2889 ships had anchored at Singapore, 383 of them owned and commanded by Europeans. They totalled 161,000 tons and carried merchandise worth $8 million.

In 1821 the first junks had arrived from China, followed by a fleet of Bugis trading ships from the Celebes, bringing agar-agar, ebony, camphor, pepper and edible seaweed. Behind them had come ships from Java with edible birds' nests, spices and gold dust, and from Sumatra with beeswax, elephant tusks, rhino horns and tortoise shell.

The figures for 1822 surpassed those for the previous two and a half years, with a trade value of $86 million – greater than the combined turnover of Penang and Malacca. Land prices were soaring. A few plots of ground previously considered valueless had been sold in an hour for $50,000.

New merchants were arriving, among them Syed Omar

Bin Ali al Junied, an Arab from Palembang, and Alexander Laurie Johnston, a Scot from India, who founded the first European firm in Singapore and became first Chairman of the Singapore Chamber of Commerce, while the most influential Chinese immigrant was Tan Che Sang, who built the first market. Tan had been born in Canton in about 1763 and had traded in Rhio, Penang and Malacca before reaching Singapore. He was already wealthy and as there were no banks he kept his money in metal boxes and slept among them. However, like many Chinese, he was addicted to gambling and is reputed to have cut off the tip of one little finger to remind him to stop playing when his luck was out, but even this drastic action failed to work.

Tan was a pure Chinese, but another man who built up a fortune in Singapore (and whose descendants live there to this day) was a 'baba' – the term used for a Chinese whose ancestors had intermarried with Malays. Ong Boon Tat (who has a street named after him) could trace his ancestors back two hundred years, and when he moved from Malaya to Singapore was highly respected as a merchant by the British. Since a baba was, in old fashioned parlance, a 'half-caste', it may seem curious that the British, who were normally averse to the children of mixed marriages, should repose any trust in him. In fact the British held the babas in high esteem for one reason: they loved the Malays with the warmth usually reserved for gentle, lazy but favoured children. They admired (if with a touch of apprehension) the diligence and acumen of the Chinese. So when a Chinese married a Malay the offspring was, in British eyes, a loved grandson destined to succeed beyond the wildest parental dreams. No wonder that grandfather Ong was awarded the contract as sole supplier to Christmas Island, a chit of paper on which he founded his fortune. Among other things, Ong bought a house standing in seven acres in Bukit Timah Road. He called in 'Bukit Rose', and it is still the Ong family home, standing in the largest private grounds in Singapore today.

*

The influx of emigrants, the almost indecent speed with which the island prospered, now forced Raffles to make a decision distasteful to himself as it concerned an old friend. He did not feel that Farquhar had the qualities required for a Resident of the new, booming settlement. It had been very different in the early days, but though Farquhar was popular, Raffles felt that he was weak in decision-making, and much given to favouritism. Not only was Raffles worried about Farquhar's abilities; the sordid question of money had to be considered. Farquhar was costing too much. He had, as a major, originally insisted that his appointment was temporary as he was due to leave for England, and because of this, the allowances granted to him had been more lavish than they would have been for a permanent Resident. But then Farquhar changed his mind. He thoroughly enjoyed the status and power of Resident. He cancelled his trip to England – though he did not cancel his generous temporary allowances. More than once, Raffles had politely asked him to leave. Farquhar simply ignored all letters, until finally Raffles had to dismiss him on the spot. The moment is described by Boulger:

> Farquhar refused to resign or to recognise Raffles's authority and, on the 21st of March 1823, he was summarily removed by an official notification, intimating that his resignation, dated and tendered as far back as the 23rd of October 1820, had been accepted.

It was an unhappy ending to a stout friendship, but Raffles was able to appoint his own man as Resident, John Crawfurd, an East India Company surgeon who had served with him in Java.

It took some time for Crawfurd to arrive, and during the weeks of waiting Raffles started to frame a complete set of laws for Singapore, an exercise that provides still another example of his tenacity. In the hateful atmosphere of Bencoolen he had lost three children, but now in Singapore, where he stayed for nearly nine months with Lady

Raffles, he was able to brush aside (or at least hide) his grief by immersing himself in a new legal world. As he wrote, he tried 'to provide for what Singapore may one day become'. His set of laws was a *tour de force* and stood virtually unchanged from 1823 until the Japanese overran the island more than a hundred years later. 'If for nothing else,' wrote Emily Hahn, 'it should be remembered as a feat of efficiency, the entire set of laws having been recorded and put in working order before their author took his leave, only nine months after arriving.' And framing laws for a constitution, as Raffles wrote to a friend, might have been 'a pleasant duty enough in England where you have books, hard heads and lawyers to refer to, but here by no means easy'.

It was in these laws that he tried to outlaw not only the slave trade, but slavery itself. The desire to establish a slave-free society had been gnawing at his conscience from his earliest days in the East, and after leaving Java he had, during his term of office in Bencoolen, managed to grant freedom to all imported African slaves. Now in Singapore, he was in his own small corner of the world, and there he drafted laws to stamp out slavery completely. He had already curbed it, but it had been difficult to control it *in absentia* (specially as Farquhar had had quite a few slaves of his own). His final words on the subject, written in a memorandum on his last visit to the island, brooked of no dispute:

As the condition of slavery, under any denomination whatever, cannot be recognised within the jurisdiction of the British authority, all persons who may have been so imported, transferred, or sold as slaves or slave-debtors, since the 29th of February, 1819, are entitled to claim their freedom, on application to the registrar, as hereafter provided; and it is hereby declared, that no individual can hereafter be imported for sale, transferred or sold as a slave or slave-debtor, or having his or her *fixed residence* under the protection of the British authorities at Singapore, can hereafter be considered or treated as a slave, under any denomination, colour or pretence whatever.

Had Raffles done nothing else in his life, this would have been worth living for.

Nothing, however small, escaped his attention. He banned cock-fighting and brothels (the latter not altogether successfully) and gaming houses in his Regulation IV of 1823 which decreed:

> Whoever games for money or goods shall receive eighty blows with a cudgel ... and all money or property staked shall be forfeited to government ... Whoever gambles, whether soldiers or people, shall wear the broad, heavy, wooden collar one month. In some cases the parties are to be transported.

(The regulation failed to stop gambling, at least among the Chinese, and Crawfurd later annulled the order.)

Raffles was even less successful in attempting to curb the use of opium. (In 1908 an Opium Commission including a lawyer, a doctor, a priest, and a Chinese, met 54 times and examined 94 witnesses to determine the extent of opium smoking in Singapore. One European witness told the Commission he smoked ten pipes in succession to test its effects. He reported: 'The only sensation was the devil's own thirst, a throat like a roll of blotting paper.' The Commission found that smokers were basically all Chinese men. Their recommendations, which were accepted, were that the government should control the manufacture and distribution of opium of a uniform standard to prevent adulteration and deception, that the price should be increased as a deterrent, but that government interference with the Chinese should be as small as possible.)

Raffles had one more dream dear to his heart, which he was determined would come true before he left the island.

This was the establishment of Raffles College. He was always deeply concerned with education, no doubt because of the way his own schooling had been curtailed. Two missionaries had started Singapore's first school, but Raffles proposed a grander scheme. He wanted to found a college where Malays could study Western knowledge, and Westerners could study Malay history and art. After talks with the Reverend Dr Robert Morrison, a former missionary in China, Morrison brought his Anglo-Chinese college from Malacca and incorporated it in a new college 'for the cultivation of Chinese and Malayan literature and for the moral and intellectual improvement of the archipelago and the surrounding countries'.

In June 1823 Raffles laid the foundation stone of the college, his last official act in Singapore. Crawfurd had arrived a few weeks earlier and Raffles had handed over the duties of Resident to him. Raffles was returning to Bencoolen, from where he would sail for home. He gave Abdullah the task of packing his collection of more than three hundred books and his carvings, bronzes, stuffed animals and birds, and bottles of preserved snakes and insects.

At a farewell ceremony Crawfurd presented Raffles with a silver tube containing an address signed by European, Chinese and Malay leaders, thanking him with the words: 'To your unwearied zeal, your vigilance and your comprehensive views, we owe at once the foundation and the maintenance of a settlement unparalleled for the liberality of the principles on which it has been established.'

Then Raffles put out to a ship in the harbour, followed by a flotilla of boats and sampans; the faithful Abdullah noted, 'Mr Raffles and his Lady embarked, followed by hundreds of people of all races, myself among the rest, as far as the ship. When they ascended the ship's side and the crew were raising the anchor, Mr Raffles called me to him and I went into his cabin where I observed that his face was flushed as if he had been wiping his tears.'

Raffles was still only forty-two and Singapore was still not officially recognised as a British settlement. However in March 1824 Canning for Britain and Baron Fagel for the Netherlands signed the Treaty of London under which the Dutch agreed to leave it in British hands. (At the same time the Dutch ceded Malacca and small establishments in India to England, and England gave up Bencoolen and possessions in Sumatra to the Dutch.)

Then, in August, Crawfurd negotiated a new treaty with the Sultan and Temenggong which gave full sovereignty of Singapore to the East India Company and its successors forever. The chiefs gave up all rights and titles to the island and became private individuals. In return the Sultan got an immediate payment of $33,200 and a yearly $15,600, while the Temenggong received $26,000 in cash and a yearly $8400.

Meanwhile, Raffles was nearing his end. He and Lady Raffles had had to wait months in Bencoolen for the ship that would take them to England. Finally, on 2 February 1824, they embarked in the *Fame*. That night, fifty miles out, a steward carried a candle on his way to one of the holds in which spirits were kept. He was looking for some brandy, and as he leaned over a keg, the brandy took fire like a flash. Within minutes the ship was in flames.

Two boats were lowered. The first took off the Raffles party and some crew members; the second, lowered from the other side of the ship, took off the captain and the rest of the crew. There was, in fact, a third and bigger boat, but it was too near the seat of the fire to be used. The passengers and crew of forty were saved, but Raffles lost all his maps, sketches, books and specimens, 'no less than one hundred and twenty-two cases, independent of those for immediate reference'.

The very next day, after the bedraggled and soaked party reached land, Raffles wrote in detail all that happened:

Sophia had just gone to bed, and I had thrown off half my clothes, when a cry of fire, fire! roused us from our calm content, and in five minutes the whole ship was in flames! ... Down with the boats. Where is Sophia? – Here. The children? – Here. A rope to the side. Lower Lady Raffles. Give her to me, says one; I'll take her, says the Captain. Throw the gunpowder overboard. It cannot be got at; it is in the magazine close to the fire. Stand clear of the powder. Scuttle the water-casks. Water! water! Where's Sir Stamford? Come into the boat, Nilson! Nilson, come into the boat. Push off, push off. Stand clear of the after part of the ship.

All this passed much quicker than I can write it; we pushed off, and as we did so, the flames burst out of our cabin-window, and the whole of the after part of the ship was in flames; the masts and sails now taking fire, we moved to a distance sufficient to avoid the immediate explosion; but the flames were now coming out of the main hatchway; and seeing the rest of the crew, with the Captain, still on board, we pulled back to her under the bows, so as to be more distant from the powder. As we approached we perceived that the people on board were getting into another boat on the opposite side. She pushed off; we hailed her: have you all on board? Yes, all save one. Who is he? – Johnson, sick in his cot. Can we save him? – No, impossible. The flames were issuing from the hatchway; at this moment the poor fellow, scorched, I imagine, by the flames, roared out most lustily, having run upon the deck. I will go for him, says the Captain. The two boats then came together, and we took out some persons from the Captain's boat which was overladen; he then pulled under the bowsprit of the ship, and picked the poor fellow up. Are you all safe? – Yes, we have got the man, all lives safe. Thank God!

Raffles finally arrived in England in August 1824, and bought a house in Mill Hill. He lived for only two more years, after a retirement that cannot have been very happy, though he did establish the London Zoo. However he was beset with all kinds of John Company problems. First, Farquhar arrived in London, railing about his dismissal and claiming that he was responsible for the creation of Singapore. Then in April 1826 the East India Company, while praising Raffles's thirty years in their service, demanded repayment of £22,000 in respect of charges Raffles had incurred and expenses which they disallowed. On top of this came news that a Calcutta firm remitting his property to England had failed, costing him £16,000.

On 5 July 1826, on the eve of his forty-fifth birthday, Raffles was found dead at the foot of the stairs in his home. The cause of death was recorded as apoplexy. The East India Company agreed to accept £10,000 in instalments from his widow in settlement of their claims. Raffles was buried in Hendon churchyard, but his main memorials were to be in Singapore – in Raffles Quay and Raffles Place, the Raffles Hotel and the Raffles Museum, in the Raffles College and Raffles statue. It is difficult to realise that he visited Singapore on only three occasions and the time he spent there totalled no more than a year.

4. 'Tiffin is Served'

The large number of Britons who, before 1860, sailed to Singapore to take advantage of its golden opportunities have often been criticised for being concerned only with making a fortune as quickly as possible and then, having achieved this comparatively simple aim, taking the first boat back to Britain. They did not, it is said, display any sense of loyalty to the island that Raffles had loved so well, they took all but gave nothing back, they lived 'European lives' that rarely impinged on the original inhabitants of the island out of whom they were making such handsome profits. In the pre-Victorian era, the influence of William Wilberforce, the voyages of Captain Cook, had awakened in many a liberally minded British breast a sense of guilt at Western exploitation of 'the noble savage' and as time passed the British in Singapore were often compared un-favourably with their Dutch neighbours in nearby Java. It was ironic to portray the once-hated Dutch as better colonists than the British, but it was undeniably true that while the average Briton usually planned to return home after he had lined his pockets, the Dutch, it seemed, went to Java to settle for the rest of their lives.

The criticism had nothing to do with differences in character, but was dictated by a quirk of geography. The British, drenched by heat and sweat, longed for home because in a country where the temperature never dropped below the eighties, the nearest mountain was more than two hundred miles away. In Java the merchants who sweated on the quayside from Monday to Friday could spend their weekends growing roses or petunias. They needed two blankets at night, simply because there was a cool mountain at almost every corner of the island. And those who have never spent three years without a break in Singapore before the days of air conditioning cannot imagine the thrill and excitement of shivering with cold.

Inevitably the difference in attitudes and altitudes led to a demand in Singapore for the ultimate possible luxuries. Even when engaged in the business of making a fortune, men were only satisfied with the best of every-thing, particularly as Singapore's life-style often went to the heads of men and women many of whom could never have aspired to similar positions in England. Yet, though they had servants in abundance, they complained about their creature discomforts, not realising that many were of their own making. Their houses were light and airy, but they filled them with unsuitable, heavy furniture which they had proudly shipped out to remind them of home.

They covered stone or wooden floors that could easily have been washed with Axminster or Belgian carpets that soon rotted with mildew. They covered their walls with ancient family portraits – often bought on the cheap if they did not have ancestors who had been worth painting; all were framed in heavy wood or gilt which the par-

ticularly voracious breed of local white ants soon recognised as specially tasty tidbits. In a country where one
could buy cheap, locally made cool rattan chairs, perspiring Britons shipped out dark walnut settees or armchairs
of the period, almost invariably with cushions covered in
brocade that made anyone who sat on them hotter than
ever. In the bedrooms the chairs were of a more delicate
'French' style, the sheets of fine Irish linen, the latter
destined to be ruthlessly pounded on stones behind the
memsahib's back every washday. And of course no house-
hold was complete without its canteen of silver cutlery
and plate, which turned green unless polished twice a
week.

When British wives complained that their lazy servants
often only managed half the work of a servant back home
they sometimes tended to forget that, by packing their
homes with ridiculous furniture, they were creating twice
the work.

Though Singapore was ruled from Bengal until 1867,
it managed its own day-to-day affairs without undue interference and it was during these years that the quality of
life changed as more and more adventurous spirits arrived,
even before the steamships began their regular monthly
trips from England in 1846 (with many more calling at
Singapore on their way to the Australian gold rush).

In many ways life was enviable. In 1840 Major James
Low of the Madras army, described in his diary how for
his 'moderate family' he kept a butler at $8 a month, two
under-servants at $5 each, a maid or *amah* (nurse) at $6, a
tailor at $8, a cook at the same wages, with an assistant at
$5 together with a washerman, two grooms, a grass cutter,
a sweeper, a scavenger and a waterman. 'But it must not
be imagined that comfort is ensured by the keeping of so
many servants,' wrote Low. 'On the contrary, a family is
worse served by these than it would be in England with
one third, perhaps one fourth of the number.'

Major Low was also disturbed by a lack of etiquette, for
there were no door knockers or name plates on the en-
trances to the houses, and since no one sat in the lower

storey during the forenoon (it was used chiefly for dinner during the cooler evenings), a stranger often went to the wrong house, 'and unless he makes a disagreeable use of his lungs, must be the porter of his own card upstairs and perhaps have half an hour's leisure to admire the prints and articles of bijouterie with which most parlour tables are plentifully garnished before the inmates of the house become aware of his presence.'

John Cameron, a former ship's captain who became editor of the *Straits Times*, has given us a detailed picture of a day in the life of a Singapore European during the middle of the nineteenth century. It was early to bed and early to rise – with a huge amount of food in between – for those who lived in bungalows (as all houses were called), most of them being two miles or so from the centre of the town. The day started when the 68-pounder at Fort Canning boomed at 5 am. Within the hour most men had set off on a two-mile walk or ride along the country path 'in the delicious coolness of morning'. In those days before the town spread, there could have been no more exhilarating exercise than an early morning ride on shaded paths, with glimpses of kampongs nestling behind banana trees, the children playing in front of attap huts, and everywhere the wet smell of a tropical morning. It was – it still is – paradise before the heat of the day.

The ride over, the men returned home, but there was no breakfast in sight – not yet. Every precious hour of coolness had to be used, so the men changed into loose clothes, usually a *baju*, a kind of loose coat, and pyjamas. Fortified by a cup of coffee or tea, with biscuits or fruit, they spent the next two hours reading, writing 'or lolling about the verandahs'. Three and a half hours passed between the boom of the wakening cannon and the sound of the breakfast dressing gong. Still no mention of breakfast itself though. 'A gentleman's toilette in this part of the East is not an elaborate one and a half an hour is ample time for its completion.'

Attached to the dressing room in Cameron's house was a bathroom with a brick-tiled floor containing a large jar holding sixty or seventy gallons of water. Like everyone else he stood on a small wooden grating close to the jar and with a hand bucket dashed the water over his body, finding that 'the successive shocks to the system which are obtained by the discharge of each bucketful of water seem to have a much more bracing effect than that of one sudden and continued immersion'.

Like every European, Cameron had a personal servant whose sole duty was to look after him. While Cameron bathed, his boy laid out his master's clothes for the day. At a cost of $2 a month, a Hindu barber came each morning to shave him. Breakfast was served at nine o'clock after the bell had been rung for the entire household to assemble – this being the first appearance of the ladies. Breakfast was apparently worth the long wait, usually consisting of fish, curry and rice, possibly eggs, washed down with a tumbler or so of claret, which Mr Cameron found made 'a very fair foundation on which to begin the labours of the day'.

Breakfast over, the carriages arrived at the front portico and the men were driven off to town – but not yet to work, for in a community thirsting for gossip, a quarter of an hour was usually spent going the rounds of the square to learn the latest news. 'As scarcely a day passes without the arrival of a steamer with news from England, China, India or from some interesting point in the neighbourhood, there is always ample material for an animated exchange of ideas and information.'

By ten o'clock, work had started; it continued 'in full force' until at one o'clock, the head 'boy' announced, 'Tiffin is served.' Rather regretfully, Cameron noted that 'tiffin time does not bring the luxurious abandonment to the table which it does in Java ... yet some show of a meal is in most cases made – a plate of curry and rice and some fruit'. After that, half an hour's snooze, then back to the office until 4.30, when most men made for the fives court or the cricket ground on the Esplanade.

Except on band nights, most people stayed at home after six o'clock. Everyone dressed for dinner, which was

'not the light airy meal which might reasonably be imagined from the nature of the climate; on the contrary . . .
the everyday dinner of Singapore, were it not for the
waving punkahs, the white jackets of the gentlemen and
the gauzy dresses of the ladies, the motley array of native
servants, each standing behind his master's or mistress's
chair, might not unreasonably be mistaken for some more
special occasion at home.'

Soup and fish usually preceded 'the substantials' – roast
beef or mutton, turkey or capon, with side dishes of tongue,
fowl, cutlets and a wonderful variety of vegetables. These
were invariably followed by the inevitable curry and rice,
garnished with 'all manner of sambals or native pickles
and spices'.

After the curry there was, of course, a pudding, and
after the pudding 'very good cheese', washed down with
beer. And after *that*, 'the luxuriance of the dessert –
pineapple, plantains, ducoos, mangoes, rumbutans, pome-
loes and mangosteens', followed by a cigar and a glass
or two of sherry, and a game of billiards before bed. 'Such',
Cameron noted, 'is the everyday life in Singapore.'

Curry and rice seemed to dominate every meal, no doubt
because the British in India had learned that the addition
of curry powder added the only flavour they were likely
to taste in the scrawny chickens raised on kampong scraps,
or the flavourless meat which no locals knew how to
butcher or cook properly. But the curry in Singapore
evolved into a very different dish from the curry in India.
Singapore used coconut when cooking the hot, spicy sauce,
giving it an entirely different flavour from Indian curry.
And then, because of the bountiful products of nature –
not available in India – 'sambals' were added: side dishes
which any self-respecting addict of Indian curry would
despise. In fact they made the Malay and Singapore curry
(which even today is cooked by Malays, not Chinese) into
one of the great dishes of the world for, in addition to the
chicken on the rice, everyone added small portions of up
to twenty different sambals – anything from prawns to

pineapple, from coconut to chillies. It is still the world's most soporific Sunday lunch.

Cameron also mentioned fish. The Malays had always been the fishermen of the island, though they fished the indolent way, allowing the fish to be caught in long spidery traps that one can still see off any part of Singapore's coastline. Britons soon found that the fish like *ikan meru* was as delicious as any from the North Sea, while the prawns and crabs caught off the North coast – still served as 'Johore crabs' – had a wonderful flavour of their own.

The wealthier Chinese also lived in style. The most respected of them in the mid-nineteenth century was a man known to everyone as 'Whampoa' because he was born in the town of that name near Canton. His name was actually Hoo Ah Kay, though this was seldom used. He called his business Whampoa & Co., and even in the *Government Gazette* reports of Legislative Council meetings, he was referred to as Whampoa, followed by his name in brackets.

Born in 1816, Whampoa came to Singapore in 1830 to assist his father who was already established as a ship's chandler, supplying vessels with meat, bread and vegetables. Whampoa became a major naval contractor, controlling the island's biggest bakery and an icehouse which he stocked with ice imported from America, where the manufacture and export of ice had just become a new growth industry.

The merits of cold storage of food by using snow or ice had been known for centuries, but the knowledge had been of little practical use in hot countries. Then Americans began to saw blocks of ice from frozen lakes in winter. They stored them in icehouses, sometimes below ground. It was only a short step to shipping the ice, insulated by sawdust, firstly to the southern States, and then to the tropics. By the 1850s, the Americans had invented mechanical refrigeration, producing ice in cans holding up to 300 lb of water, until the growth of the commercial refrigerator and the refrigerated ship ended the ice export market.

But Whampoa had made a fortune out of ice by then – and was also the Singapore consul for China, Russia and Japan. He built himself a magnificent residence in Serangoon Road, with hanging gardens and fruit orchards. Peacocks strutted in his aviary and he kept a menagerie which included stags and an orang-utan which drank cognac. For forty years Whampoa was one of Singapore's most lavish hosts. He kept 'open house', mainly to naval officers and diplomats.

Of course preoccupation with food was not only a sign of the *gourmand*. People ate a lot because there was little else to do. Those who hankered for 'a night out' could visit the billiard club, which was formed in 1829, or the occasional concert. The first public entertainment was held in 1831 when an Italian violinist gave a recital. It was such a success that later in the year the Madras Native Infantry band started to play weekly on the green sward facing the sea, and which later became the Esplanade. In 1832 the first hotel opened. In 1834 the yacht club was formed and held its first regatta. The first horse race was held in 1843 and cricket was first played in 1852.

In retrospect it seems to have been very comfortable, a typical example of the Briton's insistence on producing a carbon copy of his own country in even the most alien circumstances. 'Sunday without roast beef was unthinkable,' one Singaporean wrote. But of course there was a price to pay. Illness decimated families whose mothers were unwise enough to bear children. There was an unending battle against malaria, dysentery, dengue fever. The heat took a fearful toll of all but the most robust men, so that many of them returned to Britain too weary to enjoy their fortunes, as though fate had exacted a price for their rapacity.

Apart from anything else, the hospitals were primitive in the extreme, at a time when dozens of ships a year offloaded human cargoes of miserable impoverished immigrants, often riddled with diseases such as leprosy and smallpox. And there was no quarantine station. Mostly these unfortunates ended their days in one of the 'hospitals' for the poor which, in the 1830s, were nothing more than attap buildings with mud floors, squalid wooden bunks, and a row of latrines within the wards. They were dirty and fly-infested. Lepers slept next to influenza victims. Hygiene, and even the causes of many diseases, were so little understood in those days that in 1840 one medical officer claimed that malaria was caused by rotting bananas. There was some improvement in 1884 when Tan Tock Seng, a wealthy Chinese, built a hospital for the poor. Even so, no water was provided; patients washed their wounds in puddles outside. There were only a few wells at this time (indeed people had to wait until 1878 before Singapore had a proper water supply).

There were frequent epidemics of smallpox and cholera. In 1851 police stations held stocks of a cholera 'cure' to be taken in half a glass of peppermint water every fifteen minutes. The government published another 'cure' in four languages. The first step was to 'champoo' the body briskly. Then a wineglass of neat brandy and black pepper was followed by a mixture of a quarter of a pound of crushed ginger boiled in half a pint of water with some salt added. A later treatment involved inhaling the fumes of burning sulphur and nitre for hours at a time.

In three months of 1873, 357 men and women died in a cholera outbreak. A year later a quarantine station was established – just in time, for in the same month that it opened one ship brought in 1300 cholera-infected Chinese coolies. It took time to improve standards of hygiene, to increase medical knowledge, to plan more stringent segregation of cases, and as late as 1902 759 people died of cholera (though beri-beri was virtually stamped out by 1884 and did not reappear until the Japanese occupation).

The hazards of life on the island were compounded by the violence of both animals and men. The rats had long since disappeared (except by the Singapore River) and so had the centipedes, but in the middle of the nineteenth century an average of one person a day was being killed by tigers or crocodiles. Tigers were a growing menace in the town as the jungle was cut back for new roads and plantations. (All manner of crops were being tried at this time, from vanilla to cinnamon.) In 1839 the government offered a reward of $50 for every tiger destroyed, and this was later doubled to $100.

Professional tiger hunters, living on this bounty, came into existence, their leader being a French-Canadian named Carrol who could be recognised by a long, grey beard in which he wore a gold ring like a Scout woggle. By 1843 Europeans had formed a Tiger Club to hunt the wild cats as a sport, and the *Singapore Free Press* described an early shoot after a tiger had fallen into a 34-foot deep pit that had been prepared as a trap. The tiger hunters converged on the spot on horses, in carriages, and began shooting. When the smoke cleared it seemed as though the tiger had been killed and 'as he did not move, a dapper little man, Mr W. H. Read, got a long bamboo and gave him a prod. There was a terrible roar and a great stampede of nearly all the sportsmen helter-skelter through the brushwood in all directions.'

Yet another hazard threatened the pioneer settlers – fire. In 1830, at the time of the Chinese New Year, a fire raged in the town centre for three days after a Chinese had overturned his cooking pot in his shop in Circular Road. The blaze was aggravated when a neighbouring Chinese, who had some barrels of gunpowder in his shop, threw them down a well – in theory a good idea, but in practice unfortunate as the well was dry. The gunpowder exploded, hurling debris across the road, starting new fires which raged down Philip Street and one side of Market Street. Soldiers and convicts stood shoulder to shoulder passing buckets of water, for there were no fire engines in Singapore until 1846, and no professional fire brigade until 1888.

These hazards were part and parcel of a pioneer's life. Far worse were the dangers from men, particularly from those who ran amok. Cases were so frequent that the police force – 19 strong in Raffles's day – had grown to 130 within twenty years. Yet the police were often powerless against amoks.

In 1855 a Bugis rushed into the town centre early one evening with a *kris* in each hand. Troops fired on him but though wounded he eluded pursuit and reached the river. He threw one kris away, gripped the other in his teeth and jumped into the water. Some soldiers chased him in boats, others fired from the bank. Men who ran amok seemed to become charged with phenomenal strength and he swam underwater and escaped, to emerge an hour later from a canal. When he was cornered he charged, but then suddenly collapsed and died.

At least amoks involved only one man; gang robberies brought an added and greater terror. In 1831 a gang attacked the Reverend Samuel Milton, a missionary, who was living with his wife and two children in the Singapore Institution that Raffles founded. Between twenty and thirty raiders with blackened faces, armed with spears and axes, attacked the rooms occupied by the Miltons. They splintered the door with an axe. The missionary blocked the doorway with a chest of drawers and repelled the raiders for a time with a long. pole, while his Chinese servant, stationed beside the door, hit any heads he could reach with an iron bar until wounded by a spear. The thieves withdrew, but then returned with broken slabs of paving which they hurled through the doorway to force Milton back. Luckily, a neighbour, hearing the noise, arrived with servants and policemen.

The marauding gangs grew in size. In 1846 nearly fifty Chinese surrounded the home of a merchant, William McMicking. He met them with two pistols in his hands but was cut to the ground by a knife. One of the attackers was stooping over him for the death blow when a Chinese woman servant, with remarkable presence of mind, demanded, 'Are you going to waste your time cutting the throat of a dead man while his house is yet unplundered?' The raiders turned to looting and McMicking lived.

Later that year a gang of about two hundred attacked the home of Thomas Hewetson, clerk to the magistrates.

Hewetson fought a delaying action, shooting through the door, while his family fled through a trapdoor into the loft. Hewetson was also lucky; rescue arrived in time. When the police arrested scores of men, they found they had nowhere to put them. True, there was a jail, but for years it had been subsiding into the swampy ground, and by the time poor Hewetson was fighting for his life, it had sunk so far that all prisoners had to be confined in what had originally been the upper storey. After this a new jail was built.

The Hewetson raid, though unimportant in itself was significant in the history of Singapore because it was the first time the police became aware of Chinese secret societies – and their power. For it was the Chinese secret societies, intent on enforcing their own discipline among Chinese, who quickly told the police the names and whereabouts of the three ringleaders. The number of Chinese on the island, nearly all men, was increasing rapidly, even though British troops used Singapore from 1839 to 1842 as a base from which to fight China in the opium wars. The Chinese controlled the gambling, opium and toddy industries – all potential sources of trouble.

It was a Chinese secret society that in 1846 started the first of what became known as the Chinese riots. The head of one society, the Hoeys, had died, and his followers planned a huge funeral procession. The police banned their plans, and limited the procession to 100 who had to follow a prescribed route. The Chinese refused to obey. On the day of the funeral, 6000 followed the coffin and ignored the authorised route. Troops had to be called out.

Rioting became more frequent. In 1854 a battle between the Tu Chews and the Hokiens began with a commonplace dispute in the market place over the weight of some rice. Blows followed. The respective 'clans' or 'tribes' (as the Europeans called them) joined in. Shops and warehouses closed as the battle raged through the streets. The Governor, Colonel William Butterworth, rode into the streets on a white horse to restore calm, but was carried away after being hit by a stone. A detachment of marines was landed from a ship, and residents, together with officers from ships in the harbour, were sworn in as special constables. The fighting spread into the kampongs of the countryside. Hundreds were killed, their heads being chopped off and borne on spears. Houses were burned and looted. The rioting lasted ten days, ending in a last stand between 150 Chinese and the forces; but it was three weeks before shops reopened and normal life returned. About 600 died in the fighting, 250 were put on trial. Two were hanged, 64 sentenced to hard labour and 8 transported. And almost immediately afterwards the Singapore Volunteer Rifles were formed to aid regular troops in the event of more rioting.

The pity is that many of the Chinese troubles were due to misunderstandings, as when in 1857 magistrates were given the power to impose fines of up to 500 rupees for a number of offences including illicit gambling. To the Chinese, gambling was a way of life; they could not understand why the Europeans were opposed to it. Unfortunately they also misunderstood the law; believing that the penalty was inflexible, that anyone found guilty of gambling would be fined 500 rupees. It was, of course, a maximum fine. In protest, the Chinese closed shops, cutting off food supplies. The military and the Volunteer Rifles were called out and some residents moved their families to Java for safety. The riot ended as quickly as it began after the Governor, now Edmund Blundell, discovered the cause. He called leading Chinese merchants together and explained the act to them; he also addressed a meeting in the street. The shops reopened the same day.

The Chinese, understandably, were more involved in misunderstandings than other races. There were more of them. They had more money than other locals. They were in business in a bigger way. But, alas, they were inevitably often totally bemused by the strange ways of the British *tuans*, never more so than when the government stepped in to try and help the thousands of Singapore Chinese who regularly remitted some of their hard-earned wages to their families in mainland China. There were two ways in which they did this – by sending the money with a trustworthy friend travelling home, or by entrusting it to a professional 'letter-handler' who acted as courier and delivered money and letters for a commission. Whenever a junk was due to leave Singapore for China the harbour area would be packed with Chinese clutching their savings.

A secondary trade sprang up from this Chinese thrift – that of the letter-writer. Many Chinese were illiterate and so employed the services of letter-writers who had stalls in the city centre, consisting of little more than a stool and a table on which they set out ink, a brush and a pad of paper. The customer squatted beside the writer and dictated. The number of letter-writers doubled when a junk was preparing to depart. Many clerks earned themselves extra money by setting up in business in the harbour area, frequently with no more than a piece of board as a table.

Then in 1879 the government opened a special sub-post office to handle Chinese business and announced that in due course, as soon as it had been properly established, it would become compulsory for all mail and money for China to be transmitted through it. This was, in fact, no different from the system in use in England, and British officials regarded such a monopoly as perfectly normal. But as so often happened they did not explain their reasons to the Chinese who feared that the post office would mulct them of their savings. The Chinese letter-handlers protested vehemently. A poster denounced the 'English barbarians' for a plan that would 'injure and destroy the living of the people and produce misery beyond description'. It continued:

Alas for our coolies, with their toil, labour and miserable condition! If, after toiling with their hands or bearing heavy burdens, they have saved a dollar or two which they wish to send to their family halls to assist in providing fire and water, they cannot get enough to fill the mouth, how much less can they hope to be able to fill the caverns of this vicious and insatiable lust for gain. We must clearly awake to this vicious and delusive system, so as to clear ourselves from a guilt which cannot be prayed for.

Then came the crunch: 'As for you who wish to establish this Post Office, may your wife and daughter, dressed in their finery, be placed at the door for men to buy and deride and for the use of every lustful person ... If any honest, virtuous man will cut off the heads of the Post Office farmers he will be rewarded.'

After this incitement the new post office was wrecked, police were attacked and several Chinese were killed. The protest ended when soldiers took the Chinese letter-collectors deemed to be the instigators and imprisoned them on a ship three miles offshore. After which Noel Trotter, the postmaster-general, reopened the post office. (By 1880 it was dealing with 80,000 Chinese letters. By 1886 the number had doubled, and by 1889 the number was 280,000.)

The British officials – often as obtuse then as others could be in later years – must bear responsibility for the lack of liaison between Europeans and Chinese. Only British officials could blithely pretend to run a country in which there were thousands of Chinese without speaking their language. Yet it is an incredible fact that there was no official interpreter until Walter Pickering was appointed to the post in 1871. Five years later he became the first official Protector of Chinese and devoted himself not only to improving relations between Chinese and Europeans but to ending the exploitation of Chinese by their own countrymen. Several attempts were made on his life; he was a pioneer in the creation of today's multi-racial Singapore.

Violence also spread on the water. The islands and rivers provided natural shelters for the pirates swarming off Singapore, with their 56-foot long *prahus*, powered by eighteen pairs of oars worked by prisoners, as well as by vast sails. The ships mounted half a dozen guns and the long-haired pirates were merciless; after they killed forty-three crew and passengers on one opium-carrying junk, Bugis traders claimed that their livelihood was in jeopardy and if the government did not act forcefully they would leave Singapore. Warships despatched to Singapore were unsuccessful: so were four armed junks which Chinese merchants bought. In 1835 a public meeting in Singapore protested at the continued piracy, but they were not smashed for several more years. Then HMS *Albatross* discovered a fleet of more than a hundred *prahus*, crewed by more than 3000 men, and shot them out of the water. After that piracy diminished, though even as late as 1909 a junk on her way to China was boarded by pirates and five of the crew were murdered.

Yet, despite the violence, commerce continued to boom; between 1823 and 1857 trade multiplied five times, and the harbour was always busy, even after the British Government withdrew the East India Company's monopoly of the China trade in 1833. By this time the merchants of Singapore were well established and prosperous, thanks in large measure to the Singapore Chamber of Commerce which had been founded in 1837 and had succeeded in defeating an Indian government plan to impose import duties; Singapore remained a free port.

Businessmen arrived in Singapore from many countries, by many different routes and often by chance. Thomas Owen Crane set off from England in 1825 for India, but was wrecked off the coast of Spain. He swam to the shore where he lived for a month, according to his account, on shellfish, rats and shoe-leather, until he was rescued – by a ship that happened to be bound for Singapore. Once there, he founded Crane Brothers, a firm of auctioneers and land owners, making a fortune at a time when Raffles Square was still largely swamp.

'Daddy' Abrams, who founded the Abrams Horse Repository, which later became the Abrams Motor Hiring and Transport Co., simply crossed the causeway from Johore, where he had been in the service of the Sultan as a horse dealer and trainer.

Jose d'Almeida was a surgeon on a Portuguese warship which called at Singapore in the 1820s. He liked the island and settled, opening a shop in the square and also experimenting with all manner of crops.

Marriages between pioneer families begat new Singaporeans, born on the island, who carried on the firms. For example, d'Almeida had nineteen or twenty children. His eldest daughter married Crane. Crane, in turn, fathered fourteen children, one of whom married Thomas Dunman, who arrived in Singapore in 1842 and became Commissioner of police.

There was no lack of characters – including the man who built Singapore's first dry dock. He was Captain William Cloughton from Hull, who had realised the need for a dry dock when he called at Singapore as master of the Armenian-owned opium brigs trading between China and India. In 1854 he settled in Singapore and began the building with his savings and the investments of friends.

He was forty-three, a short thick-set eccentric. Every morning he inspected progress in the docks, always dressed in white calico pyjamas and a pith helmet, and carrying a stout stick. As he walked about a servant traipsed after him with endless cups of tea. If the tea was cold Cloughton would, without a word, box the unfortunate man's ears. Each afternoon Cloughton drove to his office in a carriage pulled by two piebald horses. For these journeys he wore a navy-blue suit with brass buttons and a black silk hat, and carried a fly whisk. He was always accompanied by a black factotum named Babo, who had once been his bosun.

In 1842 a Malay began making riding whips from gutta percha, a tree sap that was the forerunner of rubber, and its uses grew rapidly in a thriving export trade. New buildings continued to rise – though not always to the occasion, as when Captain Faber of the Madras Engineers built a bridge in 1844 with such a low span that ships could not pass beneath it at high tide. When this was pointed out to him he suggested dredging the river bed.

Faber also built a new market, the walls of which cracked, and a covered landing stage by the river, the roof of which collapsed. Even so, the name Faber is still respected in Singapore.

By the late 1850s the residents of Singapore were demanding a change in the way the island was governed. A public meeting in 1857 sent a petition to Parliament in London complaining that Bengal was too remote from the island and that, since the East India Company's monopoly had ended, it had lost interest in Singapore. Change came. In 1867 Singapore became a Crown Colony administered from London. A separate Malay Civil Service was set up and a legislative council on the island included representatives of leading merchants. The transition was marked by festivities as a new chapter in Singapore's history opened.

5. The Last Years of Peace

From the moment in 1869 when the Suez Canal opened – two years after Singapore had become a Crown Colony – the era of the steamship brought unbounded prosperity to the little island which really was (to use the hackneyed phrase) at the crossroads of the East. In the first three years after de Lesseps opened the Canal, tonnage of ships using the port of Singapore leapt from 200,000 to 700,000. Soon there were three miles of wharves at Tanjong Pagar.

When Kipling visited Singapore in 1889 he found 'five solid miles of masts and funnels along the waterfront'. He also found the roads choked with traffic, an assorted mixture of steam trams, bullock carts, horse-drawn gharries, and the first rickshaw pullers who had arrived from Shanghai. It was chaotic, even before the first motor car arrived in 1896, a Benz, known affectionately to residents as 'the coffee machine'.

This remarkable tiller-steered vehicle, with intimidating hot-tube ignition, was owned by Charles Burton Buckley, a lawyer who also wrote the *Anecdotal History of Old Times in Singapore*, published in London in 1902. He paid £16 for the car, never cleaned or maintained it, and had to push it up hills. (Within a few years there were two more cars, an Albion and a De Dion Bouton, both equally noisy. Mrs G. M. Dare became Singapore's first lady motorist and trained Hassan bin Mohamed, the first Malay chauffeur. By 1907 Singapore had an Automobile Club with a membership ranging from Buckley and his 5 hp 'coffee machine' to the Sultan of Johore and his 70 hp Mercedes.)

The congested traffic – long before the turn of the century – was directly responsible for the opening of several new hotels and restaurants. In the 1880s when the amenities of the Cricket and Swimming Clubs were confined to vigorous exercise, businessmen started to grumble at the lack of restaurants near the quays where most of them worked. In the old days it had not mattered; most men were driven home for lunch, but because of the traffic it had long since become a chore too tiresome to contemplate – particularly when a businessman who owned a large house facing the waterfront (and who boasted that he had the finest cook in Singapore) decided to open a 'tiffin room' at lunchtime, though only to selected (and paying) acquaintances. His lunches were the best in Singapore, and those who wished could eat in the garden with its chattering mynah birds, the tables shaded by scarlet flame trees and half a dozen slender, straight travellers' palms with glimpses of the sea through their delicate fan-shaped fronds. There was never a spare table and one had to phone three days in advance (on the ancient phones that had reached Singapore by 1879) to be sure of a reservation.

This was the birth of Raffles Hotel, the most nostalgically named hostelry in the world. The house was later bought and enlarged by three Armenian brothers named Sarkie, who made it the centre of Singapore's social life. Its fame was not fleeting. The *London Sphere* named it

'The Savoy of Singapore'. When Somerset Maugham stayed there, he found that 'it stands for all the fables of the exotic East', while Kipling had more down-to-earth advice: 'Feed at Raffles when visiting Singapore'. Kipling forbore to mention that it was wise to keep a sharp lookout, for only a year or two before his visit, Mr C. M. Phillips, headmaster of the neighbouring Raffles Institution, was playing billiards there when a mighty roar caused him to miscue. There was a tiger under the billiard table.

Raffles had originally opened its doors for the convenience of British businessmen, and soon other nationalities were forming their own clubs or restaurants where they could meet informally among their own kind. One such building stood out among all the others, the Teutonia Club, built by the rapidly increasing members of the German colony. They wanted a building to remind them of home, and when the Teutonia opened, it resembled nothing so much as a model of a castle on the Rhine. Built on a small rise off Orchard Road, it was described as a 'handsome building which puts in the shade any similar institution in Singapore'. Its most imposing feature was an impressive tower, quite unlike any other architectural fantasy in the city. The scene of gala balls and musical evenings, the Teutonia finally became another of Singapore's most famous hotels – the Goodwood Park.

As the hotels became more popular, clubs widened their horizons. Soon the Cricket Club started offering teas. People would meet there after listening to the weekly band concerts on the Esplanade (with tigers always in mind, from the safety of their carriages which formed a circle round the bandstand). Before the turn of the century there were flourishing polo and football clubs, and a golf club was opened in 1891. Mr Justice Goldney, dressed most unsuitably for the occasion in a red coat and a bowler hat, drove the first ball off the first tee.

But Raffles Hotel was still the centre of attraction, particularly for morning coffee on Sundays, for it was near the cathedral which had been opened for services in 1861. St Andrew's was built entirely by convict labour and for more than a century its walls have withstood all the ravages that a tropical climate struggles to inflict on men and material, due to an extraordinary plaster that made the walls so hard it is still difficult to drive a nail into them.

Lime was the foundation, but instead of mixing it with sand, the convicts mixed it with the whites of eggs and coarse sugar, beaten to form a paste. This in turn was mixed with water in which the husks of coconuts had been soaked for days. After the plaster had been applied and had dried, the convicts rubbed it with rock crystal until the walls shone and sparkled and were as smooth to the touch as marble.

The people of Singapore were far too busy making money (and enjoying themselves in the process) to worry about Singapore's ability to defend itself against attack. Attack from where? And from whom? In the eyes of the inhabitants any money spent on defence was money wasted – the more so as they knew that it would have to come out of their pockets. 'The government is spending too much of our money on defence,' cried an editorial in the local newspaper. As far back as 1861, it was a familiar cry. Indeed, the people of Singapore took a malicious pleasure when the military made asses of themselves, as they did in 1862, by which time Forts Canning, Fullerton, Palmer and Faber had been built and equipped with thirty-six guns to command the harbour and river, and Singapore had a garrison of just over a thousand men. On the Queen's birthday in 1862 the garrison of Fort Canning was to fire a royal salute from their seven 68-pounders.

At 6 am the royal standard was unfurled. Spectators clasped hands over their ears as they waited for the first gun to boom. It failed to fire. So did the second . . . and the third. Only the fourth, sixth and seventh guns fired, and the salute had to be completed with these guns. Embarrassed artillery officers never did give a satisfactory explanation for the fiasco.

As though Singapore were blessed by some divine instinct for doing the right thing at the right moment, the advent of the steamship, that transformed it into one of the world's most flourishing *entrepot* ports, was followed by two events that changed its commercial history. With the wharves, docks, ships big enough to handle any cargoes available, Singapore almost overnight became the focal point through which were channelled two products the world was suddenly clamouring for – tin and rubber.

The Straits Trading Company had built a smelter at Pulau Brani in Malaya as far back as 1890, and within five years it was producing a third of Malaya's output of tin. Then, suddenly, the demand increased. At the same time, Henry Ridley, director of the Singapore Botanical Gardens, persuaded Chinese to sow rubber seeds from Kew Gardens on plantations in Malacca. Singapore became the shipping point. The two industries of tin and rubber, added to the export of pineapples and coconuts, were to make Singapore one of the greatest ports in the world.

New faces appeared to join the perspiring British *tuans*. Many visitors stayed on impulse, like the twenty-two-year-old Iraqi from Isfahan called Saul Nassim Mashaal, who had taken a sea trip to improve his poor health and by chance arrived in Singapore in 1900 on the last day of the fast of Ramadan. There were many Moslems in Singapore and young Saul was horrified to learn that there was not a date for sale on the island – and for centuries every good Moslem had by tradition broken the fast of Ramadan with dates. Dates had never been heard of, much less grown, in Singapore. Young Saul went ashore, rented rooms over a coffin-maker's shop at the corner of Bencoolen Street and Wilkie Road and set up a modest business as an importer of dates. His business thrived. He opened a shop in Change Alley. And in 1908 his son, whose name was anglicised, was born. He was David Marshall, destined to become a barrister and Singapore's first Chief Minister.

Within a few years of the birth of David Marshall, Ong Boon Tat, who had long since moved into 'Bukit Rose' (and had consolidated his fortune), had a son who was also destined to become one of Singapore's most able barristers; he was a baba with English overtones, for T. W. Ong was educated at an English public school and took his degree at Cambridge and at the Sorbonne in Paris. A few years later another boy destined for the bar was born. He was the great-grandson of a Chinese called Lee Bok Soon, who had arrived in Singapore soon after Raffles. When he realised that death was imminent, great-grandfather Lee returned to Kwangtung province, for like many another Singapore Chinese in those days, his dearest wish was to die in his homeland. His wife, however, insisted on remaining in Singapore, because their son Lee Hoon Leong, who had started work with a shipping company as an agent, had risen to become managing director, and had no intention of leaving. *His* son, Lee Chin Koon, worked for an oil company; he was twenty and his wife, Chua Jim Neo, was only sixteen when their first child was born at Kampong Java Road, Singapore, on 16 September 1923. They named him Kuan Yew or 'Light that Shines'. As Chua Jim Neo was the great-granddaughter of a Malay woman, Lee Kuan Yew was a baba, and by a curious coincidence was later to work in the same lawyer's office as another baba, T. W. Ong.

The First World War came and went with little impact in Singapore, except for one sensation when an Indian regiment about to embark for Hong Kong in 1915 mutinied.

At 3 pm on 15 February, Indian soldiers burst open the guard room at their camp and seized ammunition. Within minutes two British captains were shot in their quarters. Other officers and men of the Malay States Volunteer Rifles barricaded themselves in the house of the regiment's commanding officer, Colonel Martin. The mutineers – 815 men of the 5th Light Infantry – swarmed out of camp, shooting and killing a judge, an insurance agent and a telegraph company man. At 4 pm many of them reached the barracks at Tanglin, where they killed soldiers guarding a prisoner-of-war camp, and released the prisoners.

Next day 200 Europeans were sworn in as special constables. A force of nearly 200 Japanese was supplied with arms. Two lorries were turned into makeshift armoured cars. The following day a French cruiser landed 190 men to help round up the mutineers. In the days that followed, a Russian cruiser contributed 40 volunteers and a Japanese cruiser 75. Then on 21 February, the fourth battalion of the King's Own Shropshire Light Infantry arrived from Rangoon. By then 52 of the mutineers were dead and 615 were in custody; only stragglers remained to be rounded up. A court martial sentenced 41 to death; they were executed outside the jail. Yet the causes of the mutiny were never known; the findings of a court of enquiry were never published. It was as if 800 men had ran amok together.

The First World War did affect Singapore in one other way. Unemployment rose sharply for the first time in the island's history. As a direct result 10,000 Chinese accepted an offer of voluntary repatriation to China. Otherwise the Chinese stood with the British in supporting the war and contributed generously to a fund to buy fighter aircraft.

As the war ended, the people of Singapore turned their attention to the island's coming centenary; a government-appointed committee was set up in 1918 to consider how the event should be celebrated. The centenary day, Thursday 6 February 1919, was declared a public holiday and the poor were given free meals. The cathedral bells pealed. The streets and the ships in the harbour were dressed with flags. Most astonishing of all, the staid Singapore Club opened its doors to women – for one day only, of course. But the main event of the day centred round the statue of Raffles. It had first been unveiled on the Esplanade in 1887 but had now been moved, in an operation that took nearly seven weeks, to a better site in front of the town hall, and there the figure of Raffles stood, eyes looking towards the river.

Guards of honour and soldiers took up their positions first, as a shower of rain ceased, and a rainbow arched above the statue, a rainbow similar to that which Raffles himself observed in Singapore exactly a hundred years earlier. Unveiling the statue, the Governor, Sir Arthur Young, declared: 'The older the world becomes, the greater will be the place assigned in history to Sir Stamford Raffles.' A regatta followed, and nine thousand schoolchildren paraded on the race-course, before the first century of Singapore ended with fireworks.

In 1921, shortly after the termination of a British–Japanese alliance, the British Government made a decision that was to have a shattering impact on the future of Singapore, and indeed of all South-East Asia, for it was a decision that instilled in British minds an unwavering belief that Singapore would become impregnable, and consequently bred an entirely new concept of military strategy in the Far East, all of it based on painfully wrong assumptions. This was the establishment of the naval base which, when ready, would enable Britain to move huge naval forces into the area. With the base, and 15-inch guns on Singapore Island, none would dare to attack the mightiest fortress in the East.

Because of world depression, the base took seventeen years to build, and work proceeded fitfully, gathering momentum during the 1930s, by which time Singapore had become a seething polyglot city of 567,433 people; according to the 1931 census 447,741 lived in the town proper, which was a bewildering mixture of old and new. In the narrow streets rickshaws and bullock carts struggled against bicycles and cars – and the sound of bicycle bells was to the streets of Singapore what taxi horns were to the streets of Paris.

The 'rickshaw wallahs' – who, because of the physical demands of their work, rarely survived more than ten years of work – provided the greatest hazard. As Singapore-born Roland Braddell wrote in his book *The Lights of Singapore*:

The rickshaw coolies still speak no known tongue. If you want to tell them where to go you grunt hard, then point; if you don't know where the place is God help you, because the coolie won't. He'll run off somewhere where he thinks you may want to go and grin happily when he finds he's guessed wrong, after which he'll run off somewhere else and grin happily again, and so on until you and your temper are entirely lost. But please don't hit him or kick him as I too often see people doing; he can't help it and he really is the cheeriest, best-humoured, most hard-working schoolboy of a fellow.

Cheek by jowl with the rickshaws, there was now a modern railway station and a modern airport with a green glass tower. It was a unique airport only two miles from the heart of the town – unique because it was built on more than 300 acres of reclaimed swampland (like so much of Singapore). Workmen had cut 200,000 tons of earth a month from hills four miles away to build it in the biggest town project since the construction of the port just before the First World War. There was even a private seaplane club whose craft were moored in the bay opposite the Yacht Club. And the RAF had a field at Seletar.

In the harbour the sampans were still propelled by Chinese standing up in their craft, dressed in faded blue jackets and shin-length trousers and straw hats. But off-shore, beyond the berths of the P & O liners, flying boats bobbed at anchor.

Though the island was still principally a fortified British base for colonial trade, the nature of that trade had changed. In 1836 74.1 per cent of imports and 67.8 per cent of exports consisted of foodstuffs, drinks, opium, tobacco and textile goods. By 1936 55 per cent of imports and 79.8 per cent of exports were in tin ore, rubber and liquid fuel. For by this time Malaya was producing nearly half of the world's output of tin and rubber, while the British and European textile industry had been eclipsed by Japanese cottons and artificial silks, on which the Singapore merchants, loyal to their established customers, imposed quotas.

Singapore's best customer had become America, which by 1938 was buying 40.7 per cent of Malaya's rubber and 54.9 per cent of its tin. (Britain bought 18.7 per cent of the rubber and 6.8 per cent of the tin.) The turnover in the miles of warehouses remained brisk. By the 1930s the port was handling some 45,000 vessels a year totalling more than 30,000,000 tons, compared with just over 2000 ships totalling 172,225 tons a century earlier.

Even in the 1930s, fortunes were easy to make (though one had to work hard as well as play hard) and the city itself was irresistible, a compound of all races, so that wherever you walked you stumbled on extravagant contrasts. In Chinatown, with its tiny shops selling lacquered ducks, flat as pancakes, or birds' nests and sharks' fins, families pecked at their lunch with chopsticks by the side of the narrow streets of tall, thin buildings that looked as though they were bedecked with flags – the coloured washing stuck out from upper windows on poles. Every day seemed to be washday in Chinatown. Yet if you turned a corner China gave way to India. The frenetic bustle of Chinese hawkers was replaced by the leisurely pace of the sub-continent, languid Indians with shirtails outside their trousers often walking hand in hand, their wives in their vivid saris. Every pavement was stained with the juice of betel nut.

Turn another corner and you came to 'white' Singapore, with all the space and greenery that Raffles had dreamed of when first he planned the city. Traffic police, wearing basketwork 'wings' strapped to their shoulders so they did not need to wave their arms in the heat, controlled the jumble of traffic. The government buildings, white and gleaming and ostentatious, gave you a sense of security. The sea greeted you at every corner (as it does today) and if not the sea, the sight and smell of the curling Singapore River, alive with sampans on which entire families were born, lived and died, never really knowing a life on land – the dances at Raffles, with women wearing long dresses, the men in short white mess jackets, known as bum freezers. Nor did they know of the great stores and institutions that had followed in the wake of expanding trade in a world apprehensive of war and so demanding the last ounce of tin, the last flat slab of latex.

In the Cold Storage building in Orchard Road perspiring *tuans*, or their wives, could buy their frozen or tinned food – baked beans, sausages, Irish stew, even 'safe' ice-cream – all nostalgic of home and England, all evoking thoughts of the next leave. In the centre of the city was Raffles Place, and in the heart of Raffles Place was Robinson's, the greatest institution of them all, a department store where you could meet friends in a new café, deliciously cool with new-fangled air conditioning. Robinson's would sell you an aspirin or a motor launch – it would sell you *anything*, and what's more would send it to the up-country planter four hundred miles to the north. There was no place like Robinson's.

Life in a duty-free paradise was so inexpensive that in some of the big hotels, such as the Adelphi, a bottle of free gin was put on the table with the pepper and salt whenever you reserved a table. Tiger beer was the local brew, but gin was still a staple ingredient of many diets. A gin *pahit* – a short drink, often nothing more than a pink gin – was popular; so was a gimlet – gin and lime served on ice. Whisky and soda was an evening drink – and consisted of only a single measure, the long glass filled to the brim: it was served in this way simply because you needed to absorb a great deal of liquid. This was the famous *stengah* – *stengah* being the Malay word for 'half'.

A dozen alleys jutted off Raffles Place, none more famous than Change Alley, leading to the waterfront, strident with the noise of portable radios babbling in English, Indian or Chinese, with Chinese and Arabs, Indians and Oriental Jews vying with each other to sell shoes and watches, torches and cutlery and the gimcrack hardware and junk of the world.

Though by the late 1930s the Chinese were far the most numerous in Singapore – 418,640 out of the total 567,433 – there were 71,177 Malays (including Javanese, Dyaks and Bugis) while the 8,147 Europeans included Americans and Canadians, Australians and New Zealanders, Russians and Swedes as well as Britons, French, Italians, Germans and Spaniards. These Europeans were the privileged class, however humble their backgrounds, however limited their accomplishments: they lived like minor princes and most of them subscribed to the advice quoted by Roland Braddell, which he said he received from his father, who received it from *his* father: 'If you want to be happy ... don't admit that you are living in an Oriental country: live as nearly as possible as you would in Europe ... Above all, never wear a *sarong* and *baju*; that's the beginning of the end.'

The British were the highest in Singapore's caste system. The lowest were the 12,000 Eurasians, products of liaisons between Europeans and Asiatics such as English and Chinese, Dutch and Malays, known contemptuously by the same word used for a small whisky – a *stengah* or 'half'. Whatever his qualifications, a Eurasian could never hope to earn more than half the salary of a European. The only exceptions were the babas, for more than a century the favourite 'children' of Britain.

But, apart from babas, a European might well have a Eurasian as a mistress (and many of the Eurasian girls were exquisite flowers), though if he married her he would be ostracised. In fact, he kept her away from the European community for he was expected to do so. Eurasians were barred from the four main white clubs. And on the *padang*, the playing fields facing the municipal offices, the Singapore Cricket Club played at one end, the Eurasian Sporting Club at the other. They were as separate as the European and Asiatic prisoners in the jail at Changi. The European prisoners lived and exercised in one wing and slept in beds; the Asians were in another wing and slept on moulded concrete slabs.

At night, when electric lights blazed advertisements for Tiger beer and cigarettes, Tiger balm cure-all pills and silk stockings in English, Chinese and Malay, the most exclusive places of entertainment were the European centres such as the Tanglin Club with dancing and swimming, or Raffles Hotel; while for bachelors there were three *kursaals*, the New World, Great World and Happy World, owned by Chinese millionaires. They provided restaurants and cabaret, theatres (with female parts played by falsetto-voiced Chinese males) and barn-like dance halls where European and Eurasian taxi dancers, as they were called, could be hired for 25 cents a dance. Round the corner were the cheaper hotels and cabarets, opium dens, gambling joints and whore houses – until the government cleaned up a notorious red light district centred on Malay Street and the brothels disappeared from *public* view, causing the American philosopher Will Rogers, returning from a visit to Singapore, to comment that the wickedest thing he found in the city was a Dutch wife in his bed (this was a long bolster used first by the Dutch; when you clasped it at night under your mosquito net, it was supposed to reduce sweating).

Though money was plentiful, nobody carried any. You signed for everything – a tin of cigarettes, a new car, even a prostitute – on the 'chit' system. Apart from the convenience (for no one wanted to carry an extra ounce of weight, even bank-notes, in the heat), it encouraged the newcomers to spend more, and, long before the advent of credit cards, the chit system was so much a part of life in Singapore that any man who regularly dodged paying for his round of drinks was never called 'stingy' or 'mean'. He was always labelled 'pencil-shy'.

But perhaps the most exciting place of all was 'home' – even if it was a home from home, for life still centred round the big old-fashioned bungalows where the 'descendants' of John Cameron lived in a modern, luxurious version of the life Cameron described so vividly in the nineteenth century. On the outskirts of town the bungalows were spaciously built to give room for the air to circulate, and set in compounds with tantalising glimpses of attap huts, palms, feathery hedges of sago, and the whisper of casuarina trees. Wherever you lived, or were invited for dinner, you were on the edge of the jungle which – or so it seemed – stubbornly refused to allow the more obnoxious concrete jungle of the city to encroach on its preserves.

Life in your home was still made pleasant by an array of servants. You could phone from the Cricket Club at 6.30 and tell your 'boy' there would be a dozen for dinner, secure in the knowledge that it would be ready the moment you reached your bungalow, and that if there were not enough plates or cutlery to go round, they would have been borrowed from neighbouring bungalows (so that often, when dining out with friends, you ate with your own knives and forks).

True, there were vague rumblings of war, and Fort Canning was no longer just a fort, but the military headquarters of a build-up of British defences – yet it was hard to take the preparations seriously while Singapore was exporting iron ore, wolfram and manganese to the Japanese to aid them in their war preparations.

And above all, there was the great naval base, finally finished by 1938. Now – even if war came to Europe – it could never come to Singapore. It had cost £60 million. Six million cubic feet of earth had been excavated, hills swept aside, a river deflected; 8,000,000 cubic feet of earth had been used to reclaim swampland before construction had even started. Out of nothing a vast base had arisen, with oil tanks holding a million gallons of fuel, with machine shops, underground munition dumps, dry docks, graving docks, giant cranes, a floating dock so big that 60,000 men could stand on its bottom. There were 22 square miles of deep sea anchorage. It was a self-contained town for thousands of men, with cinemas, churches, even seventeen football fields.

Above all else – above niggling doubts that at times

refused to be banished – this was Britain's symbol of supremacy in the Far East, Britain's guarantee that the 'arsenal of democracy' would remain safe and secure to continue producing rubber and tin for the rest of the world if the threat of war between Britain and Germany should become reality.

Is it any wonder that Singapore danced on as Europe erupted in 1939, blissfully unaware that it was heading for the greatest and most humiliating defeat in the history of British arms?

Not everyone on the island was blinkered. 'Buck' Buckeridge of the Singapore Fire Brigade had been put in charge of the newly formed AFS – the Auxiliary Fire Service. It was led by Buck, who was a professional, but manned mostly by volunteers, all training, just in case. Buck was in his thirties and had worked with the London Fire Brigade before starting a new life in the Far East. He had a short aggressive beard which matched his determination to get things done; but it was not always easy. He had little equipment and no amount of cajoling could produce any, not even firemen's helmets.

His wife Lucy – they had been married only a year – was an executive in the accounts department of Robinson's, and she, too, could see what she remembered later as 'danger signs' – for example, the extra stores of food being ordered by long-standing customers in remote areas of Malaya, whose previous orders had hardly ever varied from month to month.

Other non-government Britons were equally concerned, particularly George Hammonds, who was assistant editor of the *Malay Tribune*. Tall but not gangling, with serious eyes behind spectacles, and forever clutching a round tin of fifty Players, George was one of those characters every polyglot city produces; a man everybody knew, part of the middle stream of the city, the sort of man who could get you a room at Raffles when there was no room to be had. Policemen, parsons, pimps – everybody knew George, with his slightly hesitant voice, and everybody was envious of him when they first saw Karen, his Eurasian wife, whose Danish father and Siamese mother had produced a stunningly beautiful mixture of two handsome races. George Hammonds, now thirty-five, had fallen madly in love with her when he had arrived in Singapore ten years previously, had married her right away and cheerfully resigned from the Tanglin Club, an all-white stronghold where her presence was unwanted.

Hammonds had seen a good deal of the soldiers who constituted the Singapore garrison. There were over 88,000 of them, who crowded the Singapore dance halls when on leave. On several tours up-country he had found only a few who were 'jungle trained'. And there was not a single tank on the island. He knew, too, that the great 15-inch guns that faced out to sea and were supposed to 'guarantee' the safety of the island, would be totally ineffective against land targets as their only ammunition consisted of armour-piercing shells. Even worse, the supporting 9.2-inch guns had only 30 rounds each. Since Whitehall reckoned that – if invested – Singapore would have to hold out for six months before naval relief could arrive, this meant that in the event of a siege the gunners would be in the ludicrous position of being able to fire only one shell each six days.

Hammonds had made it his business to study the history of vacillation, inter-service quarrels, stupidity throughout the years from 1925 when the service chiefs in London had met to discuss the best ways of protecting Singapore's growing new naval base. It had all started then – with the Navy and Army wanting heavy fixed armaments to repel an attack from the sea, and the Air Force proposing the use of aircraft, which they claimed could attack an enemy before it came within range of the big guns.

The Navy and Army had won – and this had precipitated an inter-service quarrel so bitter that by 1929, when Hammonds attended military conferences, he had to travel five miles between the Army and RAF headquarters, while, incredibly, the Navy headquarters were fifteen miles from the city. There was virtually no co-operation between the services. The Army had insisted that no enemy could ever advance by land down the Malay peninsula. The RAF had a different conception, and as early as 1936 had started constructing airfields up-country, without properly consulting the Army, which would have to defend them. The Army was furious. George remembered one angry brigadier shouting that 'Some of the bloody airfields can't even be defended. The damn fools have built them in the wrong places.'

In June 1940, the picture underwent a startling change with the collapse of France. Until this moment Britain had always relied on a French fleet in the Mediterranean to contain the Italian Navy, allowing British warships to patrol Far Eastern waters. Now Britain was dramatically faced with the need to keep her fleet in the Mediterranean, leaving the defence of Malaya to land and air forces. At long last Whitehall turned to the RAF – they had no other choice – and gave a promise that 366 first-line aircraft would be available in Malaya by the end of 1941. They also decided – in October 1940 – to do something about the inter-service jealousy, by appointing Air Chief Marshal Sir Robert Brooke-Popham Commander-in-Chief, Far East.

Brooke-Popham was sixty-three. He had served with the RAF in the First World War and in 1937 had become Governor of Kenya, only to be reinstated on the active list in 1939. The news of his appointment reached Singapore editors before his terms of reference were made public, and consequently the first brief announcement did much to cheer up those 'in the know', for the bitterness between the services was an open secret. This was exactly what was needed – a man of seniority to dominate the other personalities and heal the wounds between the services.

George Hammonds would never forget his sense of dismay when he was told that Brooke-Popham, far from being overall commander, would have no control over the Navy; so that, with Britain fighting a desperate war for survival in Europe, Singapore discovered itself in the ludicrous position of having two Commanders-in-Chief, each responsible to a different authority in London, while the Combined Intelligence Bureau, on which each of the three services relied for information on Japanese intentions, troop movements and so on (and which should obviously have been under the jurisdiction of the C-in-C) remained under the control of the Navy.

Brooke-Popham, in fact, was nothing more than a buffer – the unkind might say an old buffer. The two headquarters were served by an intelligence service which hardly lived up to its name. Just before the Japanese attack on Singapore, George Hammonds had gone with several spare-time ARP wardens to a lecture, where an RAF officer had insisted that there was no need to man ARP stations at night as the myopic Japanese pilots could not fly in the dark.

T. W. Ong was also worried. By now he had grown up. Cambridge and the Sorbonne were only happy memories, and by 1940, though practising at the bar, he had donned the uniform of an officer in the Singapore Volunteer Defence Force. Yet everywhere he went, every time he was on duty, he found that nobody took the threat of attack seriously. Nor were the *real* inhabitants of Singapore – the Chinese and Malays – given any proper opportunity to join up and participate in appreciable numbers.

Instead, the *tuans* prepared for the worst – 'just in case' – for, however remote, Singapore still was a limb of Britain at war. Volunteer nurses, air raid wardens, auxiliary firemen, local defence volunteers had trained for months. There had been practice brown-outs and sessions of bandage rolling. Men and women had volunteered for blood transfusions. Food for six months had been stored, medical supplies for two years. It had all been done with a will, yet it had sometimes been difficult for civilians to realise it was not just an exaggerated make-believe, for there were few visible signs of impending war. No one could be whipped into a state of anxiety when there were hardly any shelters in the streets. Despite the war raging in Europe, there was virtually no rationing. The clubs and hotels dispensed unlimited drink. There was dancing every evening, bathing every Sunday, either at the Tanglin or Swimming Club, or on the beaches facing Johore less than a mile across the Straits – a shore to be defended, but as yet unscarred by a single pill box or roll of barbed wire. True, one saw large numbers of troops, but to the civilians it seemed they had no sense of urgency. The officers dressed for dinner in their best blues; the 'other ranks' went dancing, souvenir-hunting, or queued up at Mr Mimatsu's, the Japanese photographer behind Raffles Hotel who, with eager hisses, offered cut-rate photos of groups of soldiers to be sent home to wives or sweethearts. To the European civilians it was like living in a big garrison town during peace-time manoeuvres.

And just to make doubly sure that nobody became apprehensive, politicans and military leaders reiterated almost daily – and with the same insistence displayed by Chamberlain after Munich – that there would be no war with Japan. It was all very confusing. And it was even more difficult to forget that next morning there was rubber to be tapped, tin to be mined, ships to be loaded – and money to be made.

Part Two

The End of the Myth
(1941-5)

6. War Comes to Singapore

At 1.15 am on Monday, 8 December 1941, while Singapore slept, a telephone call awoke the Governor, Sir Shenton Thomas, and banished all thoughts of sleep. General A. E. Percival, General Officer Commanding, Malaya, speaking with agitation from the military headquarters at Fort Canning, informed the Governor that the Japanese had landed at Kota Bharu, on the east coast near the Siamese border.

'Well,' replied Shenton Thomas, 'I suppose you'll shove the little men off!' Awakening his wife and the servants, Thomas ordered coffee, and despatched a message to his Colonial Secretary warning him to stand by. Only when he had phoned several other departmental heads did the Governor scramble into a pair of slacks and an open-necked shirt, while his wife poured out a much-needed cup of coffee which they sipped on the large first-floor balcony of Government House where they normally breakfasted.

Here, for a few moments, they enjoyed their last glimpse of Singapore at peace. In the bright moonlight, the great glowing port and city were spread out before them, looking like an old-fashioned, slightly indistinct etching. The lights of the streets blinked in the hot air, and towards the centre it was possible to distinguish the silhouettes of the Cathay Building (Singapore's only skyscraper) and the white Municipal Buildings in a ring of brighter light. Beyond, the moon played on the still harbour crowded with dozens of vessels of all sizes.

Shenton Thomas had at this time been Governor for seven years after an honourable, if unexciting, career in the Colonial Service, and he was now approaching the time of retirement. Of average height, he was beginning to put on a little weight, but in a way this suited him, especially in his starched drill uniform with its white cockaded topee. He rather prided himself on 'being easy to get on with'. He liked being liked. He had always believed that it was the duty of the white man to look after the interests of 'the natives', and though he appreciated the trappings of high office (which included a yacht), he was not pompous. If he had a fault, it was a tendency to be over-optimistic.

Below the verandah the grass, bathed in moonlight, looked so inviting that Shenton Thomas descended the broad staircase and strolled out on to the lawns in front of Government House. He was still pacing between the flower beds when at four in the morning the telephone rang again. Air Vice-Marshal C. W. H. Pulford, who commanded the RAF, wanted to speak to the Governor. He had news as terse and frightening as Percival's. Hostile aircraft were approaching Singapore. They were already within 25 miles of the city. The Governor had barely time to telephone the Harbour Board and the Air Raid Precautions before the first bombs came crashing down at exactly 4.15 am.

The raid, by seventeen planes, was not big and, possibly because the street lights remained on, thousands of bewildered Chinese, Tamils, Malays – together with hundreds of Europeans – refused to believe this was anything but another practice alert. An Englishwoman who lived above her dress shop near Raffles Place had been hurled out of her bed by the blast from a bomb, but when she phoned the police and cried, 'There's a raid on!' the officer soothed her by saying it must be a practice; at which she retorted, 'If it is, they're overdoing it – Robinson's has just been hit!'

Long before dawn, the raid was over. Sixty-one people had been killed and 133 injured. Most of the bombs had fallen in Chinatown, though one had scored a direct hit on Robinson's new air-conditioned restaurant in Raffles Place, and another had shaken the police headquarters in New Bridge Road, where 'Dickie' Dickinson, Inspector-General of Police, was going about his methodical task of seizing 45 suspicious Japanese fighting vessels and rounding up every one of the 1200 Japanese on whom he could lay his hands (including Mr Mimatsu, the 'official' photographer to the forces who, it transpired, was a First World War colonel seconded to Singapore to photograph troops).

Dickinson 'called it a night' around 7 am and drove home for a shower and breakfast. So did George Hammonds, who had been working through the night on a special edition of the *Tribune*; which did not, however, include one item of news which had not yet been released — news of such staggering and world-shattering significance that it was, by a strange twist of irony, to relegate the coming struggle for Singapore to secondary importance in the global strategy of the war. The Japanese had attacked Pearl Harbor.

When the radio broke the news at breakfast time, the entry of the United States into the war was received with profound relief, and the feeling of elation was doubtless reinforced by the first war communiqué issued from General Headquarters in Singapore.

Briefly this announced that the Japanese attempt to land at Kota Bharu had been repelled. A few hours later a second communiqué spread the story that only a few bombs had been dropped on an airfield outside the town without casualties. Crowding round the briefing officer for his copy of the communiqué, George Hammonds read the reassuring words: 'All surface craft are retiring at high speed, and the few troops left on the beach are being heavily machine-gunned.'

The truth was significantly different. The beaches at Kota Bharu had been bathed in moonlight when shortly after midnight three transports anchored two miles off-shore. Almost immediately the sparsely held defences were being shelled by the attacking warships. Within the hour the first Japanese landing craft were making for the shore. The defenders fought magnificently and

though the Japanese captured two strong points before
dawn after heavy hand-to-hand fighting, this first and
crucial battle in the Malayan campaign was by no means
lost until everything was changed by a sudden disaster.
British forces were still holding the vital airfield outside
the town when a rumour swept the lines that the Japanese
had broken through and were at the perimeter. It was
quite untrue, but some unauthorised person gave instructions to evacuate the airfield. Within a matter of
hours Kota Bharu was in enemy hands. It was an ominous
preface to the panic and disorder to come.

The bare bones of the situation were that the High
Command had been caught on the hop, just as thousands
of miles away the Americans had suffered a similar fate
at Pearl Harbor, and the High Command naturally
enough was doing its utmost to cover up in the hope of
better news to come.

Of all this the civilians in Singapore knew nothing – in
fact, after they had read the communiqués the news
looked good on the first Monday of war, even though a
number of uneasy questions were already being asked.
What, for instance, had happened to the street lights during the raid? Why had they not been put out? And why
hadn't the British night fighters gone into action? Since
the High Command must obviously have known about the
Japanese landings shortly after one o'clock, and had been
presumably on the alert, how had it been possible for
Japanese bombers to penetrate to within 25 miles of
Singapore without any advance warnings?

The actual situation had been as follows: Pulford of
the RAF had warned the Governor at 4 am that hostile
aircraft were approaching Singapore, which gave Shenton
Thomas only 15 minutes to alert the city. Yet Air Vice-
Marshal Maltby, Pulford's 'number two', later admitted
that the RAF had had 30 minutes' warning of the raid.
Nobody has ever explained the mystery of the lost 15
minutes. With only 15 minutes' warning it would have
been impossible to order a crash black-out in Singapore.

Part of the city was lit by gas lamps operated by men with old-fashioned poles. Some districts had their own electric installations. There was no central switch, and in any event, the ARP was not on a war footing. Its leaders were in bed asleep – as on any other night of peace. And it was also true that all the 'top brass' – the Commander-in-Chief, the Commanders of the three services, the Governor, the Colonial Secretary, all spent the hours after 1 am discussing the landings at Kota Bharu – and not one of them thought of ordering a black-out, because not one of them thought a raid was remotely possible, since the nearest Japanese airfields were 600 miles distant in Indo-China.

Since the raid was made by only seventeen Japanese planes, many people in Singapore felt that a few night fighters taking off from the main airfield of Seletar could have quickly broken up the attack. Unknown to them, three Buffalos of the Royal Australian Air Force actually had been alerted and warmed up. The pilots had been eager to take on what one of them was later to describe as 'the most perfect night-fighter target which I have ever seen'. Permission to take off was, however, refused at the last moment by RAF headquarters, apparently because the RAF did not trust the AA gunners, some not yet blooded in warfare, and feared they might in their enthusiasm have shot at our planes. So night fighters did not go up.

Barely a week previously the Navy had been on show when the *Prince of Wales* and the *Repulse* had arrived, with not a carrier to guard them. Indeed, all that could be mustered were three cruisers, four destroyers, and some smaller craft. Few people on the island realised that these two great warships had been ordered to Singapore by Churchill against the express advice of the Admiralty, who had urged him to despatch instead a larger fleet of older battleships. Churchill, however, had insisted on sending the new ships because of 'the tremendous political effect of a really modern ship in the Far East'. He had at

least agreed that they should have air support and the
carrier *Indomitable* had been detailed to attend them.
Unfortunately she had run aground just as she was about
to sail for Far Eastern waters. Notwithstanding this setback to his plans, Churchill had insisted that the *Prince
of Wales* and *Repulse* should sail for Singapore – without
air cover.

Now, even though the nearest Japanese troops were
400 miles to the north, war had come to Singapore 'by
airmail', as George Hammonds facetiously told Karen,
who immediately went in search of black-out material.
Robinson's was crowded, and it took her an hour to get
near the counter. All around her frenzied women were
begging for black-out material. There was plenty – the
trouble was lack of assistants. Some were clearing up the
bomb debris; others collected the remnants of the
furniture from the bombed restaurant on the top floor.

People solved their black-out problems in different
ways. In her flat at Amber Mansions, Karen Hammonds
blacked out the dining room by covering the windows
and openings with brocaded Indian shawls which George
had planned to take as gifts on his next leave in Europe.

Above all, in the first days of war, people tried, almost
desperately, to emulate London's motto of 'business as
usual'. It became a point of honour not to let the
Japanese interfere more than necessary with work – and,
for that matter, play. On the Tuesday, George and Karen
Hammonds went dancing at Raffles. Normally an expensive evening out at Raffles was 'an event', and the
Hammonds had been invited, but all day Karen had
hated the idea of leaving her daughter and baby son;
George, however, felt that now, in this crisis, it was
supremely important for the white man to show the Asian
he was not afraid, though he realised that this was something that Karen with her mixed blood perhaps couldn't
quite understand. In fact George felt 'even more scared
than Karen, but I had to insist – I knew the people were
watching us and would take their lead from the way we
behaved.'

The evening was a dreary flop. Few preparations had been made to brown-out the vast verandah where Dan Hopkin's orchestra on its raised dais was playing old-fashioned dance music. The lights were so dim that the only illumination seemed to be provided by the moon-light. A few couples struggled gallantly through a series of slow fox-trots and there was a certain amount of forced humour as couples bumped into each other ('Oh! I *knew* it would be you with those big feet!') and the men with the aid of pencil torches tried to distinguish which chit they had to sign.

Relief – and an excuse to go home – came only when the sirens sounded. Every waiter bolted (allowing more than one shadowy figure to swig from the whisky bottles left on the table) and Karen began to feel terrified about the children at home. As they drove down Stamford Road, however, the all-clear sounded – it had been a false alarm – and when they reached Amber Mansions, it was to find the children asleep, and the *amah* sitting on the floor in the dark, wearing George's tin helmet. Living in a flat, George could do nothing about making an im-provised shelter, so he decided that the next morning he would buy a dozen mattresses and pile them around the dining-room table as splinter protection.

'Buck' Buckeridge of the AFS had a different kind of problem. He was short of helmets. Every demand had been refused. Two requisitions had been put in months ago to the Colonial office; no helmets had arrived. So Buckeridge decided on more unorthodox tactics. Tugging on his bristling goatee beard, as he always did when worried, Buckeridge waited for the all-clear then con-fessed his problem to a Swiss friend who ran an import business, and who had a week previously told Buckeridge, with typical Swiss caution, that he *might* be able to lay his hands on a small shipment of helmets if war came. Buckeridge told him that war had definitely come – and discovered that the foreign-made helmets were there, awaiting shipment to Siam. With some pride, the Swiss businessman produced one – and for a moment Buckeridge was taken aback. It was exactly like a German helmet. But of course it couldn't matter less. The only thing that did matter was getting helmets for his men. He sent a lorry to collect them.

Already in the initial days of war there were even more instances of the way in which the civilians would be let down by the authorities, often by pettiness that was doomed to break up any coherent action, and in which Duff Cooper, Chancellor of the Duchy of Lancaster, who had arrived in Singapore on 9 September, was to figure prominently. He had been sent out originally to study ways of improving co-ordination in the vast territories under the British flag in the Far East.

The outbreak of war had changed the picture completely, and on the Wednesday – three days after the first Japanese landings – Churchill sent Duff Cooper a personal telegram which elevated him to Resident Minister for Far Eastern Affairs with cabinet rank. His task was to include settling emergency matters on the spot when (in Churchill's words) 'time does not permit of reference home'; but his terms of reference warned him that he was in no way to 'impair the existing responsibilities' of the Commanders-in-Chief or government representatives, who would still deal directly with their departments in Whitehall.

Apparently Duff Cooper had other ideas. He now found himself President of a War Council which met daily, and he presided over the first meeting on Wednesday evening, 10 December. From that moment Duff Cooper and the Governor were sworn enemies – so much so that Shenton Thomas privately summed up to a friend their relations with the words, 'From the time of his arrival to the time of his appointment as Chairman of the War Council, he was as pleasant as could be; thereafter he was exactly the reverse.' Perhaps the impatient Duff Cooper had forgotten one sentence buried in Churchill's personal telegram to him: 'The successful establishment of this machinery

Sir Thomas Stamford Raffles, the man who founded Singapore, and (below) the hotel that is to many people his best known memorial.

Raffles Place in 1940, with Robinson's famous emporium on the right (it was burned down after the war). The government said it was impossible to build underground air raid shelters there because of swampy ground; but Raffles Place today (below) has a car park beneath its new gardens.

The German Club, with its distinctive tower, in 1900, before it became the Goodwood Park (below), one of Asia's most luxurious hotels.

Orchard Road at the turn of the century was bounded with nutmeg, pepper and other plantations. Today (below) it is Singapore's busiest street, with a new skyscraper hotel and, on the right, the Cold Storage.

Orchard Road may have changed but the street barbers are still
there – under the shade of a tree in 1880, and today (below),
sheltering from the sun under a modern pedestrian bridge.

Since the earliest days Singapore's famous waterfront has never ceased changing. Even between 1950 (above) and today (below), the transformation is astonishing. Only Clifford Pier remains a familiar landmark.

The skyline may change but the fundamental way of life has never varied in the last hundred years among the people who live on the crowded sampans on the Singapore River.

Everyone who lives in Singapore knows this unique scene – the handsome white government buildings, separated by a busy road lined with flame trees, and the padang (a general sports field), viewed (above) from the roof of the famous Cricket Club. In the background is the tall white memorial to those who died in the Second World War.

And (below) a face that is also familiar to everyone in Singapore – Lee Kuan Yew, the Prime Minister.

depends largely on your handling of it in these early critical days.'

Dramatically enough, the bitterness was increasing at almost the same time on that Wednesday evening as the people of Singapore were to receive the first shock from which the civilian morale was destined never fully to recover.

Unaware of the wrangling in high quarters which was to exert such a devastating influence on his own life, George Hammonds had just walked out of the long bar at the Cricket Club to the verandah overlooking the *padang*. It had been a suffocating day but dusk was falling. The Tamils were taking down the tennis backstop nets so they could mark out courts in fresh places the following morning – a simple expedient (providing the labour was cheap) to prevent brown worn patches at the base lines.

In the hot, stifling evening, the lazy fans in the big open rooms with the array of silver cups hardly stirred the enervating air. Music blared from a radio, but nobody paid any attention as the showered tennis players emerged from the locker rooms boisterously demanding long, cool drinks. Hammonds remembers that he was in a 'long chair', the sort always popular in the East, with swivelling extensions on which one could rest one's legs, and George was tired after a day at the *Tribune*. He hardly realised the music had stopped, that a voice was speaking out of the radio. It was more the sudden stop in the loud talk at the bar that brought him out of his chair, for now the room was utterly still except for one voice, announcing impersonally that the *Prince of Wales* had been sunk.

The silence continued for perhaps 30 seconds – until one old member dropped his glass; like a starting pistol, the sudden shattering noise began a pandemonium of bewildered conversation. George 'literally ran out of the club', got into his car, which was parked in the members' enclosure, and raced past Fullerton Building to the *Tribune* office, forgetting Karen, forgetting everything.

All who were in Singapore on that evening and who remember this moment, felt like Churchill who, 'In all the war ... never received a more direct shock ... As I turned over and twisted in bed the full horror of the news sank in upon me.'

What had happened? Despite a warning that he could not be guaranteed air cover, Admiral Sir Tom Phillips had decided that the two battleships with four destroyers should sail up the east coast 'looking for trouble'. He had *hoped* for air cover, plus an element of surprise because of the monsoon weather. On the 9th – Tuesday – he received a cable that 'fighter protection ... will not, repeat not, be possible'. Yet, while the heavy rain and grey skies hid the British warships they steamed on. Then the sky suddenly cleared – and immediately Phillips radioed Singapore that he had decided to return to the Naval Base. They were on their way back when Phillips received a report that the Japanese were invading the township of Kuantan, on the east coast, barely 140 miles north of Singapore. He decided to 'go in and help'. Unfortunately two unaccountable things happened. For some extraordinary reason, Phillips did not trouble to notify Singapore of his change of plans. And the report of the invasion of Kuantan was false. The Japanese pilots were offered a sitting target. Thirty-four high-level bombers and 51 torpedo bombers went in to the attack, sinking both ships with a total loss of 840 officers and men.

By now – though the civilian population did not know the worst – the tactical advantage had been lost forever. On land, British troops in Northern Malaya were falling back as the Japanese thrust inland from Kota Bharu. It did not matter how valiantly the defenders fought, this was a kind of war for which even the few seasoned troops were totally unprepared. While the British staggered under a burden of heavy equipment in blinding rain, swarms of Japanese commandeered bicycles and rode pell-mell through the rubber plantations. Often they wore nothing but shorts and singlets. They resembled the Malays so closely that to many of the British it was impossible to tell whether they were friend or foe. The Japanese by-passed the 'impenetrable jungle', moving swiftly through dripping rubber plantations or the narrow roads that linked one to another, often so silently that the British knew nothing until they were attacked from the rear or cut off. To the Japanese, the jungle or the rubber plantation presented no fears. To the British it was an unknown world of elephants, tigers, snakes, flying foxes – of unearthly noises, of buzzing insects, dripping vegetation, of humid rubber plantations, now hissing with torrential monsoon rain, which bred a damp, isolated gloom. In there the enemy could be anywhere – or everywhere.

Soon the RAF was falling back too. After systematic Japanese attacks on RAF planes – many of them re-fuelling on the ground – the RAF soon had only 50 planes fit for operations and most of these were being withdrawn from Malaya to Singapore Island. The Japanese had 530 aircraft – all of better quality. Daylight bombing of Japanese troops was stopped because our bombers could no longer be given sufficient fighter protection. As a result of this decision, Dutch air reinforcements flown in from Java were already being flown back again because they had not been trained for night bombing.

Now it was the turn of the civilians to have a taste of catastrophe.

7. The Bombing

Nothing is so calculated to lose a war as a policy by government to hide the truth from people. Lies have an uncanny habit of being found out, and with their policy of deliberate lying, the government and military in

Singapore must surely qualify for a place in the *Guinness Book of Records*. They hid the truth before war came to Malaya and that was bad enough; but now, when a war was being fought – and manifestly being lost – the lies continued, and it was this policy more than anything else which was responsible for the air of unreality that clouded Singapore during the first terrible weeks.

Though the news from up-country was increasingly depressing, its implications were so carefully masked that the people of the island continued to exist in a kind of dream world. They were in the war but not part of it. Gasping with heat, drifting uneasily from one day to the next (in much the same way as the people of Britain had done during the 'phoney war') they existed on rumours.

Despite the generals, the red tabs, the staff cars, the troops dancing and sweating in the barn-like halls of the Great World and the Happy World, there was little realisation of war. Up-country Malaya was as remote from Singapore as France had been from England in 1940, and possibly the fact that each was separated by a strip of water helped to heighten the illusion of security. And then too, the stifling, humid heat – accompanied now by spells of drenching monsoon rain – seemed to have drained away all energy, to have robbed the leaders, military and civilian alike, of all drive, even the ability to face up to facts.

But worst of all was the confusion throughout the city. Mr Gilmore, the deputy municipal engineer, was asked to dig trenches six feet wide and three feet deep on the many sports grounds in Singapore to prevent Japanese aircraft from landing. He managed to round up several hundred coolies, but when the work was half finished another official insisted that the trenches must be re-dug. If people crowded into them during a raid, Gilmore was solemnly warned, straight trenches would be easy targets for machine-gunning. The coolies filled in parts of the trenches which they had laboriously dug, and staggered the others. Mr Gilmore asked what to do with the dis-placed earth piled up on each side. He was told, 'Leave it there.' Along came another busybody, who pointed out that soft earth made ideal landing grounds for parachutists. Gilmore made arrangements to cart the earth away. His coolies had just finished this back-breaking task when along came the health authorities. Trenches in low-lying ground were breeding grounds for mosquitoes, they insisted. At first they demanded that every trench should be filled in, but after some argument, agreed they should be half-filled. Most of the dispersed earth was carted back and the bottom two feet of each trench filled in.

T. W. Ong, the barrister, who lived in the magnificent 'Bukit Rose' but was now a lieutenant in the Volunteers, was guarding important public buildings in the centre of the city. He remembers his uneasiness at 'the lack of *real* news' from the front, and his 'vague sense of guilt at the different world of Singapore'. For he could see the difference all around him.

Many foods were still unrationed; milk was still delivered each morning by the cold storage vans. People could buy two tins of food a day for each member of the family, and even the butter and meat rations were three times as large as in Britain. Eating out presented no problems, for though hotels observed two meatless days a week, this made little difference as poultry and game 'did not count'. There was still plenty of petrol, for almost everybody drew the extra allowance allotted to civil defence workers, and since many people had two cars, it was a simple matter to lay up the large one and use its generous ration for the Morris Minor. Schools went on as usual, and one which had had to be hastily evacuated from up-country now advertised that it had 're-opened in Tanglin for the benefit of anyone wanting to further the education of their children'.

Lulled by complacent communiqués, it was almost impossible for the people of Singapore to grasp the fact that in Northern Malaya the Japanese never slowed down. Time after time allied troops were annihilated by Japanese enveloping tactics. On the British side wrong decisions were made. Communications broke down.

Orders went astray. Whole pockets of troops were cut off. The first Japanese tanks appeared and 'came as a great surprise' to the British who had not one single tank in Malaya. In a jungle country where the British had insisted that tanks could never operate, the Japanese tanks moved easily between the spacious rows of rubber trees.

By Christmas half of Malaya's tin mines and a sixth of the rubber plantations were in enemy hands. The 'arsenal of democracy' was going bankrupt.

One story – more incredible than any of the others – needs to be related in this woeful catalogue of official ineptitudes. It tells of a secret meeting between General Percival, the Commanding Officer, and Brigadier Ivan Simson, his Chief Engineer.

Simson had been sent to Malaya to improve and add to the defences, but had been balked at every turn by General Percival, who seemed to have a fixation against such measures. Above everything else, Simson was most concerned about the complete lack of any defences on the north shores of Singapore Island, facing Johore. Nothing had been done, nothing was being done, despite many previous pleas. Simson felt that his only chance of persuading Percival to let him throw up defences on the north shores lay in getting the General alone, so that he could talk to him as man to man.

The opportunity arrived. At 11.30 pm on Boxing Day, 1941, Simson was on his way back from the front carrying an urgent message for Percival. During the long journey down the peninsula there had been two air raids. The Brigadier was dead-tired, grimy and unwashed, but he made his way directly to Flagstaff House, Percival's residence.

Percival was just about to go to bed, but when Simson announced that he bore an important message, Percival invited him in. Simson took off his Sam Browne and revolver and Percival offered him a whisky and soda, which Simson gratefully accepted. The Brigadier gave Percival the message – and then instead of leaving, drew a deep breath and announced that he would like to take this opportunity of a heart-to-heart talk on the subject of defences. Percival looked 'a trifle startled' but sat down and listened. Tall, thin, with two protruding teeth, Percival was a completely negative personality, and his first instinct when faced with a problem was that it couldn't be done – in direct contrast to Simson whose first thought was always, 'Well, let's try'. This was why Simson had elected to stay and risk all at this strange meeting in the dead of night, and now he spoke with the passionate eloquence of the professional. Defences were his main job. He believed implicitly in their value which history had repeatedly proved in modern war. And he had all the materials to hand.

He had the staff and materials, he said to Percival, to throw up fixed and semi-permanent defences, anti-tank defences, under-water obstacles, fire traps, mines, anchored but floating barbed wire, methods of illuminating the water at night. And since it now seemed inevitable that the Japanese would soon attack the island across the narrow straits, the matter was one of extreme urgency. But it could be done, said Simson. He could throw up defences on the north shore, covering the Johore Straits, 'and the water surface and shore line would be the main killing area'. To the Brigadier's dismay, Percival refused his pleas, but Simson – 'knowing I must not give way as the situation was so critical' – put down his whisky glass, leaned forward and said intently, 'Sir – I must emphasise the urgency of doing everything to help our troops. They're often only partially trained, they're tired and dispirited. They've been retreating for hundreds of miles.'

It had been a powerful plea. At first Simson had tried to speak as dispassionately as possible, but as the clock moved round to one in the morning and he seemed to be making no impression, Simson found it hard to control his anger, for Percival still refused to change his mind.

The two men were alone in the room and at last in desperation Simson cried, 'Look here, General – I've raised this question time after time. You've always refused. What's more, you've always refused to give me any *reasons*. At least tell me one thing – why on earth *are* you taking this stand?'

It was at this point that Percival gave his answer. 'I believe that defences of the sort you want to throw up are bad for the morale of troops and civilians.'

This was the Commanding Officer speaking, and Simson was 'frankly horrified' and remembers standing there in the room, suddenly feeling quite cold, and realising that, except for a miracle, Singapore was as good as lost. One can understand Simson's horror, and as he put on his Sam Browne, he could not forbear to make one last remark.

'Sir,' he said, 'it's going to be much worse for morale if the Japanese start running all over the island.'

Then he closed the door behind him. It was just two o'clock on the morning of 27 December.

On the first day of the New Year, the people of Singapore were plunged into a chilling awareness of reality, for this was the month of the bombs, and even to this day no historian has come near an accurate computation of the number of civilian deaths in Singapore between 1 January and the day on which the island capitulated.

In England during the heavy periods of bombing it had been a very different story; the whole population had been provided with documents. Ration- and identity-cards had made it comparatively simple to trace those who had vanished in the course of a raid. No such aids to identification existed in Singapore, however – particularly in Chinatown, whose influx of refugees from up-country was daily increasing the city's normal population of half a million. After a raid it was discovered that scores of men, women and children had simply vanished. In some of the heaviest attacks whole sections of Chinatown were obliterated and hundreds of bodies were never dug out. The hospitals and aid posts did try to keep some records, but even most of these were lost in the confusion following surrender.

From now on hardly a day was to pass without its quota of raids. Overnight Singapore became a city of bewildering contrasts. Houseboys and *amahs* stayed stolidly with their masters, insisting on serving 'formal' meals. Before men went to work each day, however, those who had no modern plumbing had, because of the coolie shortage, to dig a hole at the bottom of the garden and bury their nightsoil (as it was politely called). In the residential Tanglin area, with its up-to-date houses, a friend with a modern lavatory was a friend indeed.

Down at the docks the labour force was dwindling under the incessant strain of sirens and falling bombs. Hundreds of workers had fled with their families to villages inland. No shelters meant no labour. British troops were soon forced to unload their own gear under a hot tropical sun. As for the vital raw materials so urgently needed at home, huge stocks of rubber remained piled high on the wharves without a single man to load them into the waiting ships.

It seems incredible, but even when the news filtered through to Singapore – as it was bound to do – that the Japanese were over-running Johore, the civilian population did not seem able to grasp its implications. Even now, many preferred to believe that British troops had deliberately retreated to Johore where (so it was said in the clubs) the terrain would be 'more favourable to us'. Despite the evidence before their eyes – streams of dispirited, wounded troops in the streets of the city, the incessant bombing, the lack of any serious defences against air attacks – people did not see these latest enemy advances as Japanese victories, but more as a skilful Allied delaying action leading up to the moment where the tide of war would turn in Johore, the battlefield of our choosing.

The Chinese, however, were far more realistic. The news travelled swiftly along the Asian grapevine, with the result that suddenly, overnight, as though a secret order had gone out, an event occurred which was to shake the fortitude of white Singapore more profoundly than any raid. Every Chinese shopkeeper abruptly terminated the age-old chit system. Except in the clubs and some of the big stores, cash down was now the startling order of the day. In a city which had lived on credit since the days of Raffles, a community in which even the humblest clerks paid their bills monthly, thousands of men now literally found themselves without sufficient loose cash to buy food. The situation became so acute that the government was forced to start paying many of its employees twice a month; as an added incentive to stability, it also offered advances of up to $30 to anyone who wanted to buy food stocks. Desperately the Governor tried to restore confidence. In a circular to the Malaya Civil Service he declared: 'The day of minute papers has gone. There must be no more passing of files from one department to another, and from one officer in a department to another.'

'The announcement is about two and half years too late,' commented the *Straits Times* acidly. Yet, Singapore was a city of anomalies. Though the communiqués were still non-committal, even embarrassingly hopeful, everyone knew now that the Japanese were advancing towards Johore, so that it was no surprise when steel pylons sprouted on the *padang* of the Cricket Club as a deterrent to gliders. The Golf Club was turned into a military strong point, with anti-aircraft guns and troops in the club house. The Coconut Grove, Singapore's most fashionable night-club, closed down, together with two of the three 'Worlds'. Though the dance band at the Swimming Club had packed up and departed (leaving a notice by the stage 'We'll be back!'), the club remained a popular centre for swimming, and curry tiffin was still served on its broad verandah overlooking the pool. Indeed there was an added, if macabre, 'attraction'. As lunch was served, one could sometimes watch a raid on the docks as impersonally as if one were watching a war film. At Raffles Hotel the management had by now perfected a satisfactory black-out for its large dance room, and the orchestra still played from eight to midnight, though transport soon became a major problem, as most taxis vanished after dusk.

By day it was better, though more and more bewildered evacuees, often with children, crowded the streets, passing endlessly in dejected groups through Raffles Place as they made for Robinson's whose cellar had been turned into a makeshift restaurant – hot, but at least a shelter in itself – now frequently packed with women searching for friends evacuated from up-country. For the price of a coffee, they would wait for hours, and sure enough a friend always seemed to turn up. If one waited long enough, 'everybody' turned up at Robinson's, especially those who had fled on military orders with no money, and who now, as though turning to an old friend, went to Robinson's which had been a part of their lives since the day they had first landed in Malaya.

Lucy Buckeridge – the wife of 'Buck' Buckeridge, the AFS chief who had acquired the German-style helmets – was still working in the accounts department at Robinson's, and solved their problem. With the agreement of the manager, she opened a private 'bank' which made loans of a hundred dollars or so to those in need of 'petty cash'.

As soon as the sirens wailed, everything closed – banks, post offices, shops, private firms – but the moment the all-clear sounded it was 'business as usual' with a sort of added frenzy, as though to make up for lost time. The centre of Singapore was, oddly enough, comparatively safe, for the bombers were aiming for the docks and airfields. But it was a crazy sort of existence. The big shops calmly sold their wares during raid-free periods, but a woman setting off for Raffles Place could never be sure whether the shop would be open. Things worked – but they worked in different ways, and the result was often bewildering.

Karen Hammonds rushed home for lunch after picking up Barbara at school and noticed that her Chinese *amah* somehow looked different. It took her a couple of minutes to realise that instead of wearing the traditional white blouse, the *amah* had changed into a black one. And when Karen asked her why (for such a liberty was unheard of) the *amah* replied stolidly that it was so the Japanese pilots would not see her.

The schools had started their spring term, as Buckeridge discovered after he had received an urgent instruction to take over a girls' school in Tanglin for an extra AFS post – and arrived to discover the girls in the middle of an exam.

On Tuesday, 20 January, the Japanese stepped up the intensity of their air raids, and 81 aircraft in three waves of 27 flew leisurely over the heart of the city – with not a British plane in the air – so high that they were undisturbed by the AA guns. For the first time Orchard Road was badly damaged.

Next morning the Japanese bombers returned and this proved the heaviest raid the city had yet experienced. At least 383 people were killed and over 700 wounded, most casualties being in Chinatown. Over 100 aircraft attacked the Asiatic quarter of Beach Road where 47 shophouses were destroyed. Another bomb scored a direct hit on Clyde Terrace Market. Scores of people were burned to death when a third hit Havelock Road Market.

The personal column of the *Tribune* now began to fill with heartrending advertisements:

Mrs J. Norman Milne of Lower Perak and her two children are staying at 27 Newton Road, Singapore, and anxious for any news of her husband, Sergeant J. N. Milne.

Can anybody give news of her husband to Mrs Wong Ah Chan, c/o Maynards, Battery Road.

Will Mrs Jennie Lim please write to her sister Lamoon as soon as possible, as she is now without a home.

There were other, more bizarre advertisements. The New World was advertising in the *Tribune*, 'Non-stop dancing and cabaret and the usual dance on Sunday'. Another announced, 'For sale – European Guest House in select non-military area. Good business proposition. Reply with bank references.' The Goodwood Park Hotel still advertised itself as 'Charmingly situated. Ideal for visitors and tourists.' The Alhambra cinema offered Greta Garbo and Ramon Novarro in *Mata Hari*. The Cathay advised readers to 'fling away your troubles and have a fling at love and laughter' by watching their latest comedy.

Singapore was now on the edge of disaster, and, in terms of history, this was the moment when the great city – its normal population doubled to a million – should have been rallied under a dynamic leader with the soul of Raffles to prepare for the rigours and terrors of siege warfare and street fighting. It is easy to conjure up a picture of what might have been – the thousands of troops hurriedly throwing up defence works; the civilians – suddenly aware of the danger upon them – dropping everything to barricade the streets and fortify each corner; the issue of small arms to eager squads of men in ill-assorted uniforms, ready to defend each street and each house to the death; the coolies under fire stoically unloading precious war materials from the docks. Alas, there *was* no dynamic leader. It was all very well for Sir Shenton Thomas to broadcast:

This is total war, in which the whole population is involved. It will be grim, no doubt, but no more grim than in Britain, Russia and China, and if the people of those countries can stand up to total war, so can we ... Europeans, Indians, Chinese, Malays – we all stand together side by side, shoulder to shoulder.

But who was to direct their energies and loyalty? Who was to tell them where, when, how to fight? Who was to feed them? Who would look after their families if they left their jobs? The tragedy of Singapore was that all men of all creeds were prepared to fight but the flowery exhortations were never crystallised into direct, unified action. Troops as well as civilians were confused and insecure. For nearly two months they had been fed on pompous pronouncements. A ruthless censorship had hidden the truth from them. Never once in the campaign had loyal and patriotic men had a 'father figure' to whom they could turn and offer to help. And now, at its moment of destiny, Singapore was like a storm-tossed ship without a captain. There was no single mind, no man cast in heroic mould, to direct and control the thousands who awaited the call.

At this very moment of great urgency it actually took the service chiefs and the civil government ten whole days to thrash out an agreement on rates of pay for the desperately needed coolies. First, the problem was discussed in the Singapore War Council, where the Navy and the RAF demanded conscription of all available labour. Brigadier Simson, now also on the War Council, asked for higher wages, protection during raids and compensation for injury. The civil government inexplicably insisted that special danger pay 'was undesirable since it would lead to inflation'. After three days of argument the government agreed to some increase in wage rates and a measure of compulsion. Yet even so, it took the War Council another five days to agree on details. For now the service commanders said that they had no authority to spend money on increased rates of compensation. The Governor and the three service chiefs thereupon despatched simultaneous cables to London (where, one would have thought, a single cable would have sufficed) asking for a free hand to fix wages. On 29 January, an emergency Bill was passed in Singapore announcing the new labour conditions. But it was not until two days later, on 31 January, that Whitehall finally capitulated and gave the military authorities a free hand.

By then the Japanese were less than 30 miles away.

*

In London, Churchill, fearing the worst, asked the House of Commons for a vote of confidence on 27 January, and during the course of his survey of the war, told the Commons, 'We have had a great deal of bad news lately from the Far East, and I think it highly probable ... we shall have a great deal more. Wrapped up in this bad news will be many tales of blunders and shortcomings.'

George Hammonds heard this speech broadcast to Singapore a few hours later, sitting in the dark, listening to the radio in his flat in Amber Mansions. He turned to Karen and said, 'Churchill's given up the fight. You and the kids are off on the next ship. Don't argue.' Within a couple of days he was told by the government evacuation committee that she could go 'when you can get her on a boat'.

To all who heard it in Singapore, Churchill's sombre words – and the implications behind them – stood out like a warning beacon. Within hours the word had gone out along the grapevine. The four troopships which had recently brought in the 18th Division were due to leave. It was now or never. As though compelled by some instinctive urge for survival, the rush began by civilians to whom the larger issues of the war had now become crystallised into personal, agonising decisions that would affect lives profoundly.

All night and half the morning the docks and their approach roads had been heavily attacked by Japanese twin-engined bombers. Half the big godowns in the docks were raging fires. The smell of rubber mingled with that of burning tar and rope. Hundreds of civilians had been killed, and as carloads of women approached the ships near Collyer Quay ambulances kept their motors running while bodies were dug out of the smoking ruins. It was every woman for herself. The police and the Army had long since given up any attempt to marshal the traffic. Cars, driven by husbands or servants, just drove as far as they could – and then people walked. The roads leading to the three-mile dock area were often impassable – not only because of the congested stream of women on their way to freedom, but because they clashed head-on with convoys of army lorries, racing to get the military stores away from the docks so the ships could sail before the Japanese sank the four troopships berthed at the main wharf of the big, rectangular Empire Dock. One had a hole in her iron deck where a bomb had landed that morning, killing 26 men as the troops sweated to unload military equipment. Newly arrived soldiers of the 18th Division sat about on the dockside, lolling on their mountains of luggage and equipment. They had only just been disembarked, and all were in high spirits as they waited to go forward into an action about whose outcome they were pathetically optimistic.

In those last few hectic hours before Singapore became a beleaguered city, four ships managed to get away. Two troopships, the *West Point* and the *Wakefield*, left on the Friday, carrying a large number of European women and children and some Asians. A day later, under the tropic moon, the *Empress of Japan* prepared to leave with 1500 women and children and the *Duchess of Bedford* with 900 on board. And as the big ships sailed out – all to arrive safely at their destinations – the first tired troops of the Imperial forces were preparing to cross the causeway for the last stand in the 'fortress' they did not know was already doomed.

8. Siege and Surrender

As if to compensate for war, the first few days of February were beautiful. It was hot, but the humidity had dropped with the passing of the north-east monsoon, and now only an occasional shower washed the grimy, bomb-scarred city. The burning sun poured on an awakening tropical world that was always at its most exciting after the rains. Thousands of Java sparrows pecked away at the upturned earth of the Cricket Club *padang*; brightly-coloured birds flashed among the rubber trees. In the Botanic Gardens, monkeys gambolled almost down to the edge of Tyerall Road. And at night a bright moon shone out of a jet black sky laced with stars.

The British retreat across the causeway on the night of Friday–Saturday (30–31 January) had been such a closely guarded secret that 24 hours elapsed before Singapore woke up on the morning of Sunday 1 February, and read in the local newspapers that the island was invested. Thirty thousand troops had crossed the 1100-yard causeway, miraculously without a single casualty. The last were the Commanding Officer and the pipers of the Argyll and Sutherland Highlanders, who had fought every inch of the way from the Siamese frontier, and had by now been all but decimated. As the skirl of the pipes faded away at 8.15 am on the Saturday – when the last man was safely on the island – the causeway, which was 40 yards wide, was breached. Railways, water mains, lock gates, boulders weighing a ton or more were blown sky-high, and when the dust had cleared, the water was racing through a gap of 60 feet.

This had been the actual moment – 24 hours before Singapore realised it – when the siege of Singapore began. And yet, in the first few beautiful days that followed civilians hardly realised the difference in their lives, for this was the brief interlude between siege and assault. The Japanese had reached the causeway, yet they needed time to re-group and prepare to fall on the island, so the civilians who lived through this lull before the storm seem to have remembered not so much the daily bombing or a Singapore glittering with staff officers, but in retrospect a strange hiatus between two episodes of a tragedy.

It must have been a strange moment, for as the British and Japanese prepared for the battle, the opposing armies, with a bizarre irony, could even catch the occasional glimpse of each other. Separated by little more than a thousand yards of water, British troops could at times plainly see Japanese soldiers, walking about on the other side of the Straits. It seemed wildly impossible that this 'peace' could ever be interrupted, that the figures they could clearly make out were not law-abiding citizens of Johore.

To the people of Singapore, this was the classic beleaguered citadel of military history – stoutly defended, well prepared for siege warfare, and above all surrounded by water, across which, given a determined defence, no enemy could hope to force a passage. At first Europeans compared their role in history yet to be written with the embattled defenders of Malta and Moscow, not realising that the circumstances were completely different – that Malta was an impregnable fortress honeycombed with rocky shelters, whereas Singapore was a shelterless, swampy island; that Moscow was the heart of a country whose citizens preferred death to dishonour, whereas Singapore was a hotch-potch of many races with hundreds of thousands of people who hardly knew what the struggle was about.

Their illusions were heightened because everyone knew of the preparations which had been made for just such a moment as this. There was food for six months. Singapore's two largest cinemas, the Capitol and the Pavilion, together with other caches, had been turned into food dumps. Nine thousand cattle had been imported from Bali for slaughtering; there were 125,000 pigs on the island. Milk rationing would be unnecessary as the two large dairy herds normally kept in Johore had crossed the causeway late in January – in fact they could be seen grazing by the roadsides or on the golf course. Hong Kong had capitulated because it had had no water – but this could never happen in Singapore. It was true that 10,000,000 gallons a day normally pumped in from Johore had now been lost, but the island's three reservoirs assured the population of 17,000,000 gallons a day – more than the island was using under war conditions.

To the civilians in those early days, the feeling was one of unqualified optimism. What the military felt – or did – was, however, a very different matter. General Percival reckoned that it would take the Japanese 'at least a week' to mount an offensive against the island, and now he and his staff officers set about the complicated task of implementing an overall plan of defence to meet the three Japanese divisions across the Straits of Johore.

Singapore, 26 miles across and 14 miles from north to south, was generally undulating, much of it at that time covered with jungle or swamp, together with rubber and coconut plantations and many orchards and small market gardens. In contrast to the massive granite mountains of the mainland, the island boasted nothing higher than two hills in the centre, of which Bukit Timah was the larger, rising to just under 600 feet. Most of the population lived at the island's southern tip, while the few villages were clustered around junctions dividing the excellent roads, or near the 72 miles of coastline, much of it scarred with small creeks or rivers, frequently edged with mangrove swamps.

Percival's indifference – and his preoccupation with not upsetting morale – had been bad enough, for now it was obvious that an attack must be launched from the mainland. But still Percival did nothing positive. The truth is, of course, that Percival, despite his weak, unprepossessing appearance, was a man of extraordinary stubbornness, and as long as books are written about Singapore, historians will speculate on the character of this military leader who seemed to combine all the opposites in human nature. He had an irritating stubbornness in front of a military map; a completely negative, colourless personality when dealing with a group of men, but a career at staff college which had been brilliant. He had an ability to work out military schemes which looked excellent on paper, but which somehow frequently got bogged down in practice. Even his detractors admit he had a penetrating mind but (as Simson had discovered) he did not always take kindly to the advice of others.

On paper Percival could match the Japanese strength, for he had approximately 85,000 men to defend the island – but this was on paper only. At least 15,000 were baseline non-combatant, unarmed troops. The infantry battalions (thirteen British, six Australian, seventeen Indian, two Malay, plus two British and one Australian machine-gun battalions) with supporting artillery and 152 AA guns, were in a pitiable state. Some troops had sailed from Australia within two weeks of enlistment. Many hardly knew how to handle a gun.

Across the Straits of Johore, which varied in width from 700 to 5000 yards, General Yamashita was assembling three crack Japanese divisions – the Imperial Guards, the 5th and the 18th Divisions – the 18th having been landed unopposed in Southern Johore. All were fresh and jungle-trained. They were backed up by strong armoured forces, including tanks. They also had over 200 aircraft against one token squadron of Hurricanes – all that was left of the RAF.

As Percival saw it, he was faced with two broad alternatives. He could either spread out his men along the coast to prevent the Japanese landing on the 30 miles of northern beaches, or alternatively he could hold the coastline only thinly and keep large reserves of troops to fight the battle on Singapore Island itself. Though admitting that 'it was not possible with the forces at our disposal ... to build up a really strong coastal defence', Percival opted for the first alternative because 'the morale effect of a successful landing would be bad on the troops and on the civil population'.

With this as his broad strategy, the island was split into three areas which covered the entire coastline. The 18th British Division and the 11th Indian Division were placed in the northern area which extended along the north coast, from Changi in the east to the causeway. Gordon Bennett's 8th Australian Division was deployed in the western area. This stretched from the river Jurong in the south (but west of Singapore city) up to and including the causeway in the north. The less important southern

area was entrusted to the fortress garrison together with
locally recruited troops. There was also a small reserve
area in the centre of the island.

Possibly it did not make much difference where the
troops were placed – the British troops were soft after
weeks at sea, whereas the Australian contingent contained
many untrained troops – but what did make a difference
was yet another extraordinary decision which Percival
now took upon his own shoulders. It was one which
would rob the Australians of even the slimmest chance of
defending their coastline. So obsessed was Percival with
his disbelief that the Japanese would attack the north-east
coast that without warning he suddenly ordered Brigadier
Simson's Royal Engineers to shift vast quantities of
defence material from the north-*west* coast to the north-
east coast.

All Simson's extensive knowledge of military engineering cried out against the futility of the order. For weeks
– though he had received no direct orders from Percival –
Simson had been quietly 'stocking' the north-west shores
of Singapore Island, which 'everybody', including General
Wavell, had predicted as the main danger point owing to
the good embarkation facilities available to the enemy on
the opposite Johore shore. At suitable places the Engineers had left stocks of mines, booby traps, Lyon lights,
drums of petrol for fires at landing points, barbed wire
of all sorts, and pickets. Simson had even conceived the
idea of stripping the hundreds of derelict cars in the city
of their headlamps and batteries to light up the water and
the 'killing areas'.

Abruptly Percival ordered the Engineers to transfer
this vast quantity of materials. To Simson the order 'was
incredible. It was difficult to follow the minds of all the
responsible leaders and their staffs on the subject of
defence works.' For the north-east coast did, in fact, present insuperable problems to the Japanese if they wished
to launch an attack on the island. Simson had previously
reconnoitred the Johore shores east and west of the causeway. He had discovered that only to the west of the

causeway were there reasonable facilities and road access for embarking men, tanks, stores, for a major attack. No such facilities existed in the marshes and mangrove swamps east of the causeway. Yet there was nothing Simson could do about it. Everything had to be moved – in double-quick time. By a stupendous effort, all the defence stores were moved and dumped east of the causeway by 5 February. During that night, however, reports of heavy Japanese troop concentrations facing the north-*west* coast reached Percival, and the following morning Simson was told to move all the material back. By then, of course, it was too late.

Of all this, the civilians were, perhaps mercifully, kept in ignorance. There was, however, one fact which could not be hidden from them – the gushing, writhing, black plumes of smoke from two huge fires far to the north. They were the oil dumps at the Naval Base, and they had been burning for days. The ominous clouds had drifted across the green island and now started to darken the sky above the city itself. At first people had jumped to the conclusion that Japanese aircraft had scored two hits. But slowly, rumour began to spread that this was not the work of the Japanese, but of the British. It seemed absurd, of course, yet the stories persisted, and when Hammonds questioned his military friends who could normally be relied upon to help him, they closed up like clams – until suddenly, the truth was revealed to him in an off-the-record press conference.

The briefing room was crowded. Local newspapermen, foreign correspondents – with British, American and Australian newspapers predominating – jammed the stuffy room in the Cathay Building where staff officers sometimes held their background talks. Hammonds had been warned that the meeting promised to be historic. The briefing officer gave a few preliminary remarks ('a softening-up process', whispered the correspondent next to Hammonds) before he finally came to the point.

There had been a lot of speculation, he said (in so many words), about the fires at the Naval Base. He felt he should put the correspondents 'in the picture'. Suddenly, as Hammonds always remembered, the room full of tough newspapermen became suddenly silent and aware of impending drama, the sense of momentous news. None, however, could have guessed the whole truth – that not only had the British fired the oil dumps, but that the entire Naval Base had been evacuated by the Royal Navy. A note of despair at the useless waste creeps into George Hammonds's notes. 'Never throughout all the fighting – all the defeats – did I ever feel such a sense of utter dismay,' he wrote. 'It seemed impossible that this naval fortress which had cost £60 million and taken seventeen years to build could have been thrown away like this – without even a fight for it.'

This was Britain's great symbol of naval dominance in the Pacific Ocean, and it had been built for one reason only; for just such a moment of destiny as Britain now faced. And in all this story of equivocation, of ineptitude, of the myth so assiduously fostered, nothing can match in grim irony the fact that when the moment of destiny finally did arrive, the base was valueless and impotent.

Worse was yet to come. After a series of probing questions the briefing officer was finally forced to admit that the base had in fact been evacuated *before* the troops had crossed the causeway. 'But I thought they'd been withdrawn to the island to defend the base?' one voice asked. There was no answer. Nor could there be, for the Navy had pulled out – leaving the Japanese thousands of pounds' worth of equipment.

To the civilians a new hazard was now added to the ruthless daily bombing. Early in February the Japanese opened harassing artillery fire from the mainland. Long-range guns sited on high ground in Johore were able to bring in their range, not only the island's four airfields, but the entire city as well. And this was unlike anything else the civilians had ever imagined or expected. In a way they had become fatalistically used to the whistle of falling bombs; they had learned to take the anti-aircraft guns for granted, even the regular sight of unopposed Japanese aircraft lazily peeling away after dropping their bomb loads. The raids, too, were launched with an almost clockwork punctuality, and the civilians could tell from the whistle where the bombs were likely to fall. Few bothered to take shelter except when the raiders were directly overhead.

Now, however, an altogether more menacing element entered their lives. There was something almost inhuman about this sound which they had never heard before – a low whine in the distance that slowly crept up the scale until it became a wild, screaming noise culminating in a piercing crescendo. And no one knew where the noise would end.

Now, too, the raids were being stepped up. Using four repaired airfields in Johore, the Japanese were sending not only dive bombers but fighters to cruise low over the city, machine-gunning the streets or dropping showers of small anti-personnel bombs which burst in the air into hundreds of tiny, sharp fragments of shrapnel. The pock-marks of war showed more and more. Hardly a street did not have its gaping hole or jagged dusty ruin to mark the path of a bomb or shell, though some places seemed to bear charmed lives. The Cricket Club had only been bombed once. Robinson's was never hit again after the first night – and was to remain open for business right to the end. The Singapore Club was untouched except for shrapnel scars. But in some parts of Chinatown entire streets had been obliterated. The Singapore railway station had been badly damaged. In the nearby dock area half the godowns had gone up in flames.

By the end of the first week of the siege at least two hundred people a day were being killed – not including those whose bodies were never found. Raids could no longer always be signalled by sirens. The blue sky and the sun were obliterated by smoke from the burning oil tanks that hung over the city. Each day there was mounting evidence of an uglier mood – particularly among the troops. Bewildered knots of men wandered, leaderless, without orders. They were sprawled haphazardly all over Singapore, seemingly without anyone to direct them. Without warning, one resident found the compound of his house filled with convalescent soldiers 'who all looked hale and hearty'. One road was blocked for hour after hour because a column of troops could not find an officer to tell them which turning to take. Many troops were desperate with fatigue – but often they could not find their units and had to sleep on the floor of the YMCA after a supper of tea and buns. Others who did manage to find their commanding officers still had nowhere to sleep – because there were not enough tents, and billeting officers had been unable to requisition enough rooms. Gunners could not find their guns, army cooks could not find their raw materials. Inevitably, drunken, dishevelled troops appeared, reeling around the main squares, waving bottles of cheap liquor. (Crème-de-menthe was a great favourite.) Their mood became more bitter – and more belligerent – with each new raid or rumour.

Looting was rapidly becoming widespread. Buckeridge was clanging along to a fire when a bunch of drunks, amused by his beard, jeered, 'Let it burn, dad! It's too late.' They started to pelt him with big, oblong 'missiles', two of which landed by his side in the front seat. They turned out to be cartons of cigarettes.

In Government House, Shenton Thomas struggled to 'live according to his station'. Each morning after a breakfast – which invariably ended with toast and marmalade – the cook brought the day's menu for his approval, though lunch was now largely reduced to cold cuts. Shenton Thomas, however, insisted on guests wearing collars and ties, though he dispensed with dinner jackets in the evenings. He now faced an urgent, new personal problem. His wife had been taken seriously ill with amoebic dysentery – which meant that it was quite impossible for her to go to the shelter in the grounds. Yet the bombing raids had killed several of his staff, torn a vast hole in one corner of the enormous white 'palace', and now the Japanese guns suddenly found the range of

Government House. Firing from Johore, at 24,000 yards' range, they bombarded the Governor's residence with devastating accuracy. Lady Thomas could not leave her bed, but the Governor's ADC did the best he could. Using every spare mattress he could find, together with bales of wool sent up to Government House by the Red Cross, the ADC made a shelter of sorts under and around the big banqueting table in the formal ground-floor dining room. The small entry hole was just high enough to allow the Governor's wife to be wheeled in on a very low stretcher.

In the chaos, the civilians and a host of refugees felt more and more bewildered. Almost everything they were told seemed to be contradictory. In his 'Battle of Singapore' Order of the Day, Percival had made a great play of phrases like 'the enemy within our gate', 'loose talk' and 'rumour-mongering' – all calculated to alarm civilians (when in fact there was virtually no 'fifth column'). A few days later Wavell issued his Order of the Day, in which he said that 'our part is to gain time for the great reinforcements' which he promised would arrive. Yet in the next breath he demanded that 'we must leave nothing behind undestroyed that would be of the least service to the enemy ... I look to you all to fight this battle without further thought of retreat.' To the million bombed, shelled civilians with their backs to the sea, it was not clear how anybody could retreat from a beleaguered island, nor how the scorched earth policy which Wavell demanded would be of help to the reinforcements which he had promised were on their way.

There was no inspiration to the civilians, no direct appeal to them, no leaders to whom they could turn, no clarion calls to take up arms. While some played bridge, or quietly got drunk, others formed queues outside the cinemas. Flt. Lt. Arthur Donahue of Minnesota, the first American to fly with the RAF in Britain, was now flying one of the last Hurricanes in Singapore. He was given a couple of hours' leave after days of non-stop flying and went with some friends to *Ziegfeld Girl* at the

Alhambra Theatre. 'The shock was quite rude for us when it was over; completely lost in the lovely atmosphere of American girls and song and gaiety and peace, we stepped out into the teeming oriental traffic and the sweltering tropical sun to be reminded that we were half-way round the world from America, with our enemies only a few miles away.'

Small pleasures (or small problems) loomed larger than life. Canon A. J. Bennitt, of the cathedral, noted in his diary with satisfaction that 'the municipality fixed us a gas heater' for his hot bath. George Hammonds received his monthly bill for $4.50 from the Swimming Club and felt that 'I suppose we've got to go on supporting them but they might cut down the sub. when nobody uses the place.'

It was a curious unreal existence. There were now more soldiers than ever before on the island and despite the anticipation of impending battle – to say nothing of impending defeat – the first thing the troops did when they got an hour's leave was to buy souvenirs to take home. The small shops and stalls in the narrow, stifling Change Alley were jammed with more customers than in peacetime.

In Raffles Place, Lucy Buckeridge at Robinson's reported more over-the-counter sales than ever before – which helped to offset the collapse of their up-country trade. Round the corner in Battery Road, Mrs Lily Jackson worked on at Maynards the chemists, superintending Elizabeth Arden beauty treatments. Fraser and Neave still bottled their soda water; Tiger beer was still brewed; the brickworks carried on making bricks – while Percival was planning his scorched earth policy. When T. W. Ong went to Wearne's garage in Orchard Road to collect his car, he found the garage inundated with minor repair jobs because cattle from the dairy herds had reached the outlying districts and motorists regularly hit them in the black-out.

At night you had to book a table if you wanted to go to Raffles. The Cricket Club was filled with noisy drinkers, and many members went there directly from offices or ARP headquarters for a quick shower because the club was centrally placed. At the sole remaining 'World', a soldier had to queue for half an hour before he could get a 7d. dance with a taxi girl – unless he invested in a roll of tickets, and waved them, whereupon the girl (who got a percentage) would attach herself to him for the rest of the evening.

At 10.30 on the night of Sunday, 8 February the first Japanese troops attacked on a broad front between the two bays on the north-west coast of the island under cover of devastating artillery and mortar fire. The first Australian sentries on the Singapore shoreline spotted the boats bobbing across the black water. The alarm was given, and hundreds of Australians opened a withering fire. The first wave of enemy troops was destroyed. So were many in the second wave. Yet such success could not continue, for the Australians were fighting against one overwhelming disadvantage. According to plan, the killing area in the Strait should suddenly have become as light as day – illuminated by scores of brilliant searchlights, which were there, waiting to be switched on so the defenders could blow the enemy out of the water. Instead there was blackness everywhere, and the Australians could only fire against invisible targets. How could they be sure where the weaving small boats were? All they could see was the occasional blacker shadow against the water, all they could hear as a guide was the high whine of outboard motors. Men cursed and shouted for light as they stumbled against each other in the dark. And still the small rubber boats came on relentlessly, cloaked in blackness. And then, too, what had happened to the artillery at this critical moment? A counter-barrage had been planned for the moment of the attack. Instead, British guns remained mute.

There was a simple, tragic explanation, though the Australians defending the beaches could not know it at that time. Nobody was able to get a signal to either the searchlight teams or the guns. Long before the Japanese had begun to scramble ashore, every line of communication had been cut – and no instructions ever reached either the searchlight crews or the artillery. And without those signals they could not go into action.

Thus it was left to the infantry to send up SOS signals before a few guns opened fire – but by then the Japanese were ashore along the entire front, and before the Australians realised what was happening, they were fighting with the bayonet in the damp, sombre plantations, and the Japanese, as always, seemed to be everywhere – in front, behind, on either side, infiltrating swiftly behind disorganised pockets of Allied troops cut off from their colleagues. Swarming through the close, intricate country, each Japanese party was led by an officer with a compass strapped to his wrist. Carefully avoiding any frontal attacks, they sought out the gaps in the Australian lines and pushed through behind them. Once the Australians – who had no compasses – lost sight of the Strait and were attacked from the rear, they did not even know which direction they faced in the maze of the jungle, lit only by the stabs of light from gunfire and the occasional Japanese barge burning offshore.

By 1 am the Australians were withdrawing from their forward positions. It was a catastrophe of the first magnitude. By dawn nearly 4000 Japanese had secured a firm foothold on the island. Their forward elements were already advancing towards Tengah airfield, west of the city. And by then the High Command had issued its first communiqués, in which it announced with irritating blandness that 'Offensive action is being taken to mop up the enemy.'

By now it must have been clear to those in authority that the island was doomed. Though on the surface it would seem to have been a relatively simple matter for a beleaguered city to blow up anything that might be useful to the enemy, the situation was fraught with certain complications. The Governor was still responsible for civil affairs – and he had to consider the fact that if or when the city capitulated, many of the Asian businessmen would no doubt try to carry on as best as they could. The military naturally wanted to deny as much as possible to the enemy, but Shenton Thomas did in fact have the last word on what should, or should not, be done to the hundred or so major civil installations, and he refused to sanction the destruction of about forty Chinese-owned engineering works. There were big workshops, many equipped with the latest and most modern machinery. Others were stacked with brand new vehicles. Most of the more important Chinese engineering works were left in running order for the enemy.

The Governor's decision gave the enemy many new vehicles and well-equipped workshops, and we can only surmise the reasons behind it. Of course the Governor was rightly proud of the way in which he 'looked after the natives' who would have to carry on after any surrender. He believed Malaya was their country and that he was there to protect them (against themselves if necessary). But one must also remember that the Governor's responsibilities, though unchanged in theory, had in practice been whittled away. The war had not only swept across a country, but had swept away the cobwebs of colonial government. Slowly but relentlessly the Governor found himself becoming more and more of a figurehead, miserable at not being permitted to do more than sign unimportant papers and make 'public appearances'. Even his critics admit that Shenton Thomas was incapable of a mean action, and without any doubt he believed that the Chinese would have to 'carry on' and must be left with the means to do it – though this theory hardly tallied with the ruthless way in which all fishing boats had been smashed up or sunk.

On the other hand, few civilians attempted to defy the order to smash the liquor stocks. The horror stories of the Japanese drunken rampage in Hong Kong were too fresh in people's minds to be forgotten or ignored. Sir Shenton Thomas had not only announced that a total ban on all liquor would come into force at noon on Friday the 13th, but had ordered big firms to start smashing their stocks immediately. The Customs led the way by breaking tens of thousands of bottles of hard liquor.

All over the city, people were destroying their own precious stocks, in some cases the results of years of 'collecting'. Buckeridge was helping out at Robinson's for a day and a half – while the customers in the store had no inkling of what was happening. Chinese boys lugged case after case of whisky, gin and brandy out of Robinson's cellars into a courtyard behind the store where other boys were waiting to rip off the tops. There, a team of six men smashed the bottles in the only way possible – by hurling them one by one at a brick wall opposite. 'I never realised', wrote Buckeridge in his diary, 'just how long it takes to pull twelve bottles out of a case, then throw them against a wall.'

Something else had to be destroyed – bank notes. And this was even hotter work than smashing bottles under a blazing sun, for the notes had to be burned under the watchful eye of a senior official. The task fell to Eric Pretty, the Acting Federal Secretary. Despite the run on money, the Treasury reserves still totalled $5 million, and early one morning Pretty went to the vaults below the government offices in Empress Place, not far from Fullerton Building. In the next cellar was the furnace used by the government to destroy confidential papers. It took a day to burn the money, for though there was a fair proportion of $100 bills. 'It seemed to me', said Pretty, 'as though there were an awful lot of fives and tens.' Pretty could not just allow the messengers to toss the bundles into the furnace. Each batch had to be checked and the numbers of the notes recorded as the boys brought them in from the vaults. 'I never imagined I'd have so much money to burn,' sighed Pretty.

All this work of destruction – to say nothing of the problem of living – was being enacted against a grim background of increased shelling and bombing. Not only was Chinatown bombed ruthlessly. The Japanese now singled out Orchard Road as a target for their guns. This wide straight street was the main military link between the city and military headquarters at Fort Canning, and the Japanese regarded it as a legitimate target – despite the presence of the Cold Storage, the Municipal Market and other big shops. All day long the military traffic tore along it, running the gauntlet of the shells that whined and crashed. Half the buildings seemed to have been hit by now. Abandoned or burned-out cars littered every corner. Water gushed along the deep gullies from unmended pipes. Here and there bodies lay waiting to be collected, many of them civilians, for people had to live, they had to eat. George Hammonds, like everyone else, had to buy food. He usually went to the Municipal Market at 5.30 am parking his car at the corner of Cuppage Road. On this Tuesday there was not much to buy at the market, for only a handful of apathetic Chinese stood around in the vast hall lit by guttering candles. After buying some vegetables, George went to Robinson's to get a haircut, then walked out into Raffles Place. With the heat of a new stifling day pressing down and the bright sun already hurting his eyes, Hammonds wiped his glasses, pulled a cigarette from his round tin, and lingered on the steps of the big store for a few minutes. He remembers the scene vividly. The famous square – the real heart of white Singapore – had hardly been touched. Even the noises of war were muffled by the high buildings, and the square was filled with people of all colours – some in white ducks, some in shorts, others in sarongs – either busy or unconcerned, going in and out of shops, talking at the corners. An Indian street-trader squatting on the pathway dozed over his tray of cheap trinkets; a Malay driver was fast asleep at the wheel of a *tuan*'s parked car; a food hawker bobbed along, two containers dangling from the bamboo across his shoulders; an old, bearded white man in shorts, sports shirt and sandals came out of Kelly and Walsh, the booksellers, clutching a big new volume with a shiny cover – and was already dipping eagerly into it as he brushed past George.

The grounds of Government House – to say nothing of the city – were not only plastered with bombs, but with an incredible assortment of enemy leaflets. One bore a crudely drawn picture of a girl languishing in the arms of a soldier, with the puzzling caption, 'Nightmare of your neglected wife: "Oh, Tommy! I am going crazy."' Another announced that Singapore was rioting, that British and Australian troops were secretly evacuating the island. It urged the Asian troops to 'Pack up your troubles in your old kit bag and co-operate with the Nippon Army.' A third bore a drawing of an obese British planter lolling under a fiery sun. Yet another showed a gluttonous British officer tucking into steak and chips while his starving Indian troops looked on with drooling lips. 'Leaflet collecting' became a passion with hundreds of Chinese children who had never collected cigarette cards in their lives.

As the rate of wounded – both military and civilian – increased daily, every available building was turned into makeshift hospitals. Even St Andrew's Cathedral became a first-aid post. Chairs, pews, hymn books, hassocks were hurriedly cleared from the nave to make room for stretchers and beds. The vestry was turned into an operating theatre. Nurses and doctors moved in with bottles of antiseptic, rolls of bandages, splints and drugs.

By the 12th morale was beginning to crack. Mr V. G. Bowden, Australian government representative in Singapore, had to cable Canberra that 'a group of Australians and others' had boarded a vessel without authority and sailed for Java. The city was crowded with sullen, armed deserters 'in greater numbers' (according to *The War Against Japan*) 'than could be controlled by the Military Police'.

The next day – Friday the 13th – the crack widened, and by the afternoon there was panic at the docks. Men were shouting and yelling that they had passes and should be let through. Children and their mothers who *had* passed through the gates were sobbing because their husbands who could be seen waving *their* passes were being refused admittance. Whenever the gates were opened, there was a concerted surge towards them, and only with the utmost difficulty were the police able to close them again. The psychological effect of having got a permit to leave and then being refused permission to do so was too much for many of the desperate men. Some were crying and sobbing. Others tore at the gates in vain, trying to force them open. Still others, waving their passes, screamed abuse at the police who stood there stoically silent.

Perhaps the most tragic death of all on that terrible afternoon occurred as a young couple with their baby in arms stood waiting for their turn to pass through the gate. Their passes were in order. As the fighter-bombers swooped low over the crowd the wife was hit by a piece of shrapnel and killed instantly. Her dazed husband – standing next to her and still clutching the baby – was unharmed. At his side lay the body of his wife. In front of him was the ship that was the child's sole hope of freedom. 'Buck' Buckeridge, who had been fighting a fire on the wharf, saw it all, and wrote, 'Never have I seen a look of such agony on a man's face.' Buckeridge watched as the husband, dazed and crying, hesitated. A sailor yelled at him to come aboard. He looked back – one last glance at the body on the pavement – and then, blinded with tears, took the only decision he could take for the sake of the baby. Stumbling, he passed through the gates, leaving the mother's unburied body on the wharf.

But at least by nightfall, an armada of 44 ships – ranging from naval sloops (of a kind) to outboard motor launches – sailed south for Java. Admiral Spooner was on board. So was Air Vice-Marshal Pulford, whose last words to Percival, as he said good-bye, had been, 'I suppose you and I will be blamed for this, but God knows we've done our best with what we've been given.'

There was another – though less spectacular – evacuation that evening, this time from Government House, which by now had the air of an enormous white ghost villa. Its empty corridors echoed with the crump of bombs, the swish of shells and the bark of guns surrounding the building. By now the shelling was so severe that people hardly dared to climb the handsome staircase to the first floor. The last telephone link with the city had been cut. Many of the servants had either been killed or had fled, and though the Governor had been determined that the Japanese should not drive him from his home, he now had no alternative but to be evacuated to a new one – the Singapore Club in Fullerton Building, near Raffles Place.

Here, two of the members' bedrooms had been made ready for him – one to be shared by the Governor and Lady Thomas, the other for his small remaining staff. They enjoyed the doubtful luxury of a small shower room – doubtful because the tap only worked intermittently, and already most of the water had to be carried from a standpipe in the street. That evening the Governor had his first 'club' dinner – bully beef and tinned potato salad, washed down with tea and tinned milk – which he ate perched on the edge of his bed. Lady Thomas was too ill to take food.

Nearly a hundred VIPs were now crowding into the few bedrooms usually reserved for up-country members. Some had brought their own camp beds. Rooms normally occupied by one man now held four or five. Apart from the Governor – who took his meals in his room – everyone had to queue up for what scratch meals were available in the makeshift cafeteria.

By now even Churchill, who had demanded that every street should be defended to the end before entertaining any thoughts of capitulation, was forced to change his mind, and cabled the Commander in Chief, 'You are of course sole judge of the moment when no further result can be gained at Singapore.'

That cable marked the end of Churchill's dreams and hopes – hopes that by a heroic defence against inevitable defeat, Singapore would rank in military history with Warsaw; that instead of handing over intact this glittering symbol of Britain's colonial power, the ashes of certain defeat would provide history with a matchless epic of unyielding British courage that would echo around the world.

Among the white population, there was now a firm realisation that soon they would be interned – and that meant one final shopping spree. Canon Bennitt, who had an aversion to growing a beard even in captivity, went from shop to shop buying razor blades, a few at a time – in all, enough to give him a shave every other day for several years. There was also an unprecedented rush to the dentist's by people who felt that 'If I have to be interned, at least I didn't want toothache as well.' In some indefinable way the fear of toothache became a minor obsession, worrying able-bodied men more than the prospect of dysentery or beri-beri that were to kill hundreds.

There was a rush, too, on Kelly and Walsh, the booksellers, where half the shelves were already empty, and the big airy shop had the bleak, unwelcome look of a 'going out of business' sale. Despite the heat, a milling throng scrambled for the few books that were left, while a smiling, unfrightened Chinese girl took the money, counted change, and apologised because wrapping paper had run out.

Many shopkeepers refused money from their old and trusted customers. At Maynards the chemists, the manager insisted on thrusting upon friends toothbrushes, tubes of paste and soap. Curiously, few people bothered about buying tinned food. Perhaps instinctively they felt as Buckeridge did, 'It's going to be a bloody long stay.' And so it cannot have seemed worthwhile buying a 'luxury' that would have lasted only a few days. On the other hand, there *was* a run on one luxury – cigarettes. Even the most philosophical were dismayed at the prospect of facing up to the rigours of internment without tobacco to tide them over the first few days.

But without doubt those in the most pitiful plight were the mothers with young children. For weeks now the pathetic groups of women, mostly young, living out of one suitcase, with their children tugging at their soiled dresses, had been a daily spectacle in Singapore. Some had obstinately refused to leave without their husbands, taking heart from the spurious military communiqués. Others, who were penniless, had not realised in time that the government was ready to stake their passage money.

Now this unhappy band faced one common problem. Not for them the mad rush to buy cigarettes or toothbrushes or books. Now that internment was all but a reality, only one thing mattered: the welfare of the children. Clothes, shoes, hats against the sun, baby foods – all these had now become dire necessities. The mothers knew they could – and would – have to go without themselves. But the children – often deprived of milk and special foods – were different. And yet there was no official body to whom they could turn for help, not even a charitable organisation with a 'treasure chest' able to dole out the reach-me-downs of other, luckier children who had left.

Then, in the last hours, something very close to a miracle happened. How the word got round – how it by-passed shelled roads, torn buildings, smashed telephones – will never be known, but it did, and while the shells whizzed overhead and the fires raged round the corner, Raffles Place unaccountably became filled with excited, laughing children, suddenly decked out in their 'Sunday best'. It was an astonishing sight. Little girls pirouetted as they showed off spotless, cool, pretty white dresses. Boys proudly displayed trim shorts and white shirts. There were floppy hats and shining new sandals for everyone. In addition, each child – or its mother – carried a parcel containing a duplicate outfit – everything from underpants or panties to a spare pair of shoes. Even the mothers – still in their old, unpressed clothes – seemed to throw back their shoulders with a new surge of pride and thankfulness.

For the 'miracle' had been performed by Robinson's where the manager, Mr L. C. Hutchings, and Lucy Buckeridge (who managed to get away by one of the last ships) had decided that every European mother now facing internment could come to the store and get two free outfits for each of her children. The cost? 'Let's talk about that later,' said Robinson's.

On Sunday morning General Percival, in freshly starched uniform, attended communion at Fort Canning, and at 11.30 am despatched two emissaries to discuss surrender terms with the Japanese. They returned with a message from Yamashita. He would not order a cease-fire, he said, until Percival had 'signed on the dotted line'. And he would treat with nobody but Percival in person. Meanwhile the shelling would go on. Together with three staff officers, General Percival set off. At the approaches to the village of Bukit Timah they got out of their car, unfurled the Union Jack and the white flag, and marched under enemy escort to the Japanese headquarters – the bleak, functional Ford Motor factory.

Yamashita arrived several minutes later – and from the outset any hopes which Percival might have entertained for getting conciliatory terms vanished. Yamashita raised his voice and thumped the table. 'Are our terms acceptable or not? Things have to be done quickly. We are ready to resume firing.'

As Percival hesitated, one of Yamashita's aides pushed in front of him a list of questions in English. Percival looked at the first one: 'Does the British army surrender unconditionally?'

With 'bowed head and in a faint voice', Percival gave his consent. The surrender would take place at 8.30 that night.

9. Under Japanese Rule

In his Japanese version of the fall of Singapore, Colonel Masanobu Tsuji makes the fascinating point that he found among the conquered British 'an expression of resignation such as is shown by the losers in fierce sporting contests' and it is a curious fact that on this last night of 'freedom' – the unreal interval of suspended time between the war and captivity – all feelings of apprehension seem to have been absent. George Wade, in civilian life an expert on controlling Singapore's voracious white ants, noted in his diary: 'That night we had a steak and kidney pie, Christmas pudding and strawberries and cream, all out of a tin, for our Surrender Dinner.' Leslie Hoffman, a reporter on the *Malaya Tribune*, was surrounded by British troops who pressed on him vast stocks of tinned food – and a black Scottie dog called 'Whisky' which one of the soldiers asked him to look after – almost as though he would be returning soon to collect it.

Everyone was busy preparing their 'internment kits' – some bulky and unwieldy, since many people innocently assumed that in a climate as hot and humid as Singapore's, the Japanese would obviously have to provide transport. 'If they put us in Changi,' one woman said briskly, 'I'm not *walking* nine miles. And if I refuse to walk, they'll *have* to transport me or leave me free.' It never seemed to enter the heads of many people that if they started getting 'cheeky', the Japanese soldiers would have as little compunction in killing them as in swatting an irritating bluebottle.

Many thought of only one luxury – a bath. Buckeridge let one of his closest friends, an ARP warden called Tim Hudson, into a secret. Among the few treasures Lucy had left behind before being evacuated was a key to the private entrance used by the senior staff at Robinson's. Almost the last advice Lucy had given him was to go to Robinson's 'if the city folds up' in case he needed anything to take into internment. And only a couple of days previously one of Robinson's men had casually passed on the information that as soon as the island's reservoirs had been bombed, all the baths on sale in Robinson's plumbing department had been filled to the brim – just in case.

The stairs to the upper floors were set at the back of the store – a handsome, wide staircase that split left and right so shoppers could go up one side and down the other. A light was shining – and instinctively Buckeridge and Hudson took the left staircase, simply because it was marked 'Up'. At the top stood Mrs Hutchings, wife of the manager. 'Why! It's Lucy's husband,' she cried. 'I recognise the beard. Don't be alarmed – there's half a dozen more upstairs – though we don't want a crowd. How about a nice cuppa tea?' In the furniture department a couple of electric bulbs glowed brightly. A dozen or so men sat lounging in the deep armchairs and sofas that nobody would ever buy now. Busily Mrs Hutchings bustled from one to another with a big teapot.

Buckeridge and his friend had their baths, taking their choice from a dozen filled with water. In the ladies' hairdressing department they found some soap, then lay back in the first bath, scrubbing until the water was black, after which they washed the rest of the dirt off in a second bath.

Soon after dawn on Monday, 16 February, the first Japanese troops entered the city. Almost the first step the victors took was to ask British officials in key posts to carry on as usual. For now the Japanese unexpectedly faced overwhelming administrative problems. They had advanced 650 miles from Singora in Siam to the harbour in Singapore in 70 days – a remarkable average of nine miles a day. As a result they had so overstretched themselves that not even the most sanguine Japanese staff officers had been prepared for victory so soon.

There was only one thing to be done. The Japanese appealed to the British for help. British firemen, doctors, nurses, water engineers, health and sanitary workers were asked to remain at their posts until their Japanese counterparts arrived. Fires were still burning, wounded were still dying, water was still running to waste. And the only people in a position to restore some semblance of order were the conquered British.

Next day imprisonment began. By ten o'clock on the Tuesday morning two thousand men, together with three hundred women and children, were lined up in the blazing sun on the Cricket Club *padang*. The men were at one end, the women and children at the other. It was one of the hottest days of the year. Not even the sea, which almost lapped its edge, could provide a breeze to temper the stifling heat that beat down relentlessly on this beautiful sports ground, with the blue water on one side and the Municipal Buildings, flanked by flame trees, on the other.

This was the first batch of internees and it was a heart-rending scene. Men stood miserably by their pathetic bundles of salvaged luggage. The women, their frocks already limp with sweat, were not allowed to talk to the men, but tried desperately to hold back their tears as they made sure the children, playing cheerfully, kept on their hats against the sun. Some women had brought prams in which to carry their belongings.

In a knot slightly apart from the other men stood the senior government officials who had walked across Anderson Bridge from the Singapore Club. Sir Shenton Thomas was dressed in newly pressed clean white ducks. On the *padang*, he held his head high, for he felt (as he said later) that he was with his people, and he wanted to take his punishment as they did, without fear or favour. Already, however, he was to be singled out as 'a special case to be humiliated' for though the Japanese permitted several senior officials to be driven to the first camp, they specifically insisted that the Governor should walk the whole distance.

One man who did not go immediately into internment was 'Buck' Buckeridge, who of all the civilians experienced perhaps the least painful transition from war to 'peace'. It was not wholly painless, for as Buck wrote, 'one could never, never forget the feelings of humiliation.' But while thousands of civilians now suddenly found themselves with endless idle hours in which to think, Buckeridge was working from dawn to dusk, trying to restore order in those parts which had suffered extensive fire damage. On the very first day the Japanese had asked him to help in putting the city back on its feet, and it was a colossal task. (In fact, it was to be six months before Buckeridge was interned in Changi.)

Buckeridge had been told to tour godowns that had not been bombed, to make certain they contained nothing inflammable, and when he forced open the sliding doors of one particular godown, he exploded into a string of oaths. For there in front of his eyes was the one item of equipment for which he and the ARP chiefs had begged time and again, only to be told repeatedly that none existed in Singapore – neatly stacked rows of new helmets. They must have arrived even before the war started. 'While every civilian in Singapore had been begging for helmets, someone in authority had forgotten all about this little lot.'

With the surrender, others were in and out of prison. T. W. Ong took off his uniform and went home, but was soon sent for by the Japanese and was taken to a secret rendezvous where he was questioned for two weeks. He was beaten mercilessly – and then, just when it seemed he was about to die, he was released. A month later he was sent for again 'as a Chinese spy in the pay of the British'. Again he was brutally beaten for several weeks. Again he was released and sent home, almost dead. This treatment happened a dozen times in the years that followed.

For three and a half years thousands of men, women and a handful of children were interned on the island of Singapore. None of the civilians had the remotest chance of making a dash for freedom from a speck in the ocean as escape-proof – and as evil – as Devil's Island. And though it was hope and faith that sustained the majority, it was hard even to have any hope in those first months when it seemed that nothing on land, in the skies and on the oceans could arrest the all-victorious Japanese. Life was wretched. Malnutrition caused many deaths. So did the peculiar Japanese indifference to illness, so that, for example, chronic diabetics died simply because the Japanese refused to issue the insulin which existed in Singapore. Others died as the added privations advanced old age.

Contact between the city and the camp was not difficult if one had the nerve and courage. At first many Europeans were at liberty. But even when men like Buckeridge were interned after six months, the Japanese needed to send small but regular parties of Europeans into Singapore for a variety of reasons, and though they always went under guard, sometimes the soldiers could be bribed, while others were so lazy it was easy to deceive them.

One man who had to make frequent trips to the city was Norman Coulson, a PWD water engineer. The water system at the Changi was constantly in need of repairs and replacements – no doubt helped by a little sabotage – and Coulson, as the only expert, was detailed to buy the spare parts in Singapore. Before long he was in touch with the Chinese underground, and – through a go-between – with Leslie Hoffman, the Eurasian reporter of the *Malaya Tribune*, who was daily operating a short-wave radio he had concealed from the Japanese. In the hope that the news would seep into Changi, the British in India were broadcasting hours of morale-boosting personal items from wives, relatives, and friends of those in camp. Hoffman faithfully wrote down the simple, poignant messages – many telling a man in prison the one item of news he most wanted to know – that the wife he had evacuated was safe. The problem now arose of how to smuggle the news into camp, and Hoffman had to act with the utmost discretion, for almost immediately after capitulation he had been interrogated and beaten up by the Kempetei; and though he had been released after some weeks, he was still under suspicion. However, he and Coulson contrived an ingenious plan. Hoffman wrote the notes on rice paper. These were then delivered to a Chinese plumber, and each time Coulson visited Singapore, he was able to hide the precious messages in the pipes and joints he bought from the plumber for the ancient pumps at Changi. In all Hoffman sent several thousand messages into Changi. It was then a simple matter (comparatively simple, that is) to relay the messages from the men's to the women's camps.

The prisoners in Changi were sustained not only by a stoic acceptance of their wretched lot, but by increasing glimmers of hope – first, the news of the approaching doom of Germany, which they heard on the secret camp radio. There were also exciting local tidbits of news that concerned them more intimately, and these had come trickling into the camp through the drainpipes of Norman Coulson and Leslie Hoffman. Details were sparse, but there could be no doubt that, despite brutal Japanese reprisals, British officers were leading attacks on lonely Japanese outposts in Malaya.

On one exciting morning, news came through that 22 Japanese soldiers had been attacked and killed near Kuala Dungun by a British officer leading a party of armed Chinese. To the prisoners it seemed incredible, and 'Buck' Buckeridge remembers that when he was told, 'I found it hard to believe the news was true. Britons actually still fighting in Malaya!'

It *was* true. Throughout the years of occupation a force of determined Chinese guerillas, led by the legendary

Colonel Spencer Chapman, waged unremitting warfare on lonely pockets of Japanese troops. They were members of the famous Force 136, whose mission was to harass the Japanese. They were controlled from headquarters in Colombo, which at first despatched officers to Malaya 1700 miles distant, by submarine.

Europeans with a knowledge of Malaya and its languages directed operations; Chinese were recruited for the fieldwork, to be led by men like Lieutenant-Colonel John Davis, who arrived secretly by submarine in the Malacca Straits in 1943. With five Chinese, he paddled ashore at midnight, landing on a deserted beach. Then they headed into the jungle. Like all the British officers, Davis carried L (for lethal) tablets in case he was captured by the Japanese.

Spencer Chapman described their life in his book *The Jungle is Neutral* (1949). He lived on a diet mainly of tapioca. He suffered acute diarrhoea. He was in attacks by the Japanese. He was even captured by Japanese, but escaped, after which he made contact with Chinese guerillas, whom Britain was prepared to arm and finance. These included one brilliant jungle fighter, a born leader, a young Malayan Chinese in his twenties called Chin Peng. Like many, he was a dedicated communist, but Britain could not afford to be particular. By November 1944, Force 136 in Colombo was equipped with a squadron of Liberators, which had the range to reach Malaya. From the first tentative air drops the supply of arms, food and supplies became as regular as a bus service. In June and July 1945 there were 249 sorties to Malaya; in August and September 756. More than five hundred soldiers were infiltrated and more than seven thousand packages of arms and stores were dropped without the loss of a single aircraft.

The Force 136 officers organised the guerillas – almost all of them communists – into seven independent anti-Japanese regiments, known as groups, which were, in order of founding, Selangor, Negri Sembilan, North Johore, South Johore, Perak, West Pahang and East

Pahang. Each had a British liaison officer. Spencer Chapman's unit transmitted its first message to Colombo by dint of frantic pedalling to charge the batteries of the radio, and went on transmitting three or four hours a day, only going off the air if a Japanese aircraft was overhead.

Slowly the years of agony rolled on until men and women who could hardly remember anything other than the stifling atmosphere of the camp, suddenly began to sniff a new and heady scent – the scent of victory, of liberation. VE-Day came and went. On the secret radios, news filtered through of the massive American naval victories in the Pacific, to be followed by the details of Hiroshima, so that almost before the prisoners realised what was happening, one of the British camp doctors was startled to see a cheerful British soldier pat his Japanese guard on the back, whereupon the guard offered him a bar of chocolate. Were the rumours of Japanese surrender true? asked Cicely Williams, a doctor in the camp, whereupon the Tommy gave a reply that only a soldier could give. 'Don't worry,' he grinned. 'The Emperor's signing on the dotted line next week.'

Part Three

The Road to Independence
(1945-65)

10. The Great Illusion

No battle in history was won and then lost with such absurd anticlimaxes as the battle for Singapore. In 1942, the Japanese army, smaller than the British and shorter of ammunition, had conquered the island when hundreds of thousands of Allied troops surrendered. So unexpected was victory that Britons like Buckeridge had to be pressed into helping the Japanese to stamp out fires before being packed off to Changi.

In 1945, after the atomic bomb had been dropped, thousands of Japanese soldiers, their armies intact, their magazines bursting, their stranglehold on countries all over Asia complete, laid down their arms to a puny force of Allied soldiers. So unexpected was *their* victory that the British had to ask their one-time conquerors to help them until reinforcements arrived on the island.

Victory was followed by what afterwards came to be called 'the great illusion'. For those in Changi, the outside world had stood still for three and a half years, and as the gates of release clanged open and the bedraggled survivors inhaled the first breath of freedom, many fondly imagined that it would be a simple matter to take up life where they had left off.

The city itself helped to foster the illusion. Buckeridge remembers wondering if the Japanese had changed Singapore, pulled down buildings, erected new ones – in short, if they had left their own imprint on the great port, visually and physically. Instead he found the skyline very much as he had left it. Perhaps it was the never-changing weather – the pitiless sun, or the pelting rains of the monsoon thrashing against rattan blinds, that gave the illusion that everything was just the same. Or perhaps it was because Singapore is an island port, so that Keppel Harbour, the hot, shimmering, outlying islands, the lines of waving palms, the unchanging apparatus of dockland, the same pewter-coloured petrol tanks, were unaltered. Fullerton Building still stood on Collyer Quay; Battery Road, linking it with Raffles Place, was still as narrow as ever. The shape of the streets in the centre of the city, the squares, the sports grounds, were unchanged; Robinson's still dominated Raffles Place. Behind it the narrow, bustling Change Alley was soon thronged with troops searching for bargains or sailors searching for girls. Behind it the Singapore river was still covered with a patchwork quilt of sampans. Raucous voices cried their wares as the waterboats and food hawkers made their daily rounds. Agile, skinny Chinese still leapt from one floating family to another, past women cooking rice and fish in the same kind of coalpots, and above all, there was still the sweet and sour stink of the river, an odour giving many of the freed men and women – and the first returning residents from Europe or India – a comfortable feeling of sameness, of never really having been away.

The illusion was supported by the early enthusiasms of the Malays and Chinese. When Tim Hudson, the ARP warden, walked through the camp gates a small figure clutching a parcel elbowed her way through the dense, waiting crowd. It was his *amah*, carrying a parcel of freshly laundered clothes. 'They were still warm with the smell of a hot iron,' Tim remembers.

When George Hammonds returned from India and made his way straight to the offices of the *Tribune* some of the old typesetters were there to greet him, with tears in their eyes. And later, at the Cricket Club, the same boy who had always served him in the past was there, smiling with a *stengah* before he asked for one. 'The Japs might never have been here,' he told a friend gratefully. 'Thank God there's one place in the world that'll never change.' He lifted his glass, 'Cheers to Singapore!'

'Buck' Buckeridge experienced much the same emotions when he stepped out to freedom and then drove through the streets of the city. 'It was like a dream, as though a curtain of horror had been torn down,' he remembers. In a way he was right, but the dream that Buck saw and felt was like a second curtain – one of those beautifully painted cinema drapes that look so thick and heavy until the lights of the projector are turned on and one can see the screen through material that is flimsy, with no substance to it.

At first, naturally, any sense of change, any difference in attitudes, was masked by the exhilaration of victory, not only on the part of Britons released or returning, but by the Chinese, Malays and Indians who, though technically remaining free during the Japanese occupation, had suffered grievously under the Japanese heel.

From zealously guarded secret caches, forbidden Chinese fireworks were soon crackling with a sound ominously like that of machine-gun fire; and most intriguing of all, the city – small streets as well as large – was almost immediately bedecked with thousands of Union Jacks, hidden for more than three years (many of them, it has to be said, by the same people who had been so ready in 1942 with the flags of the rising sun).

In the first flush of exuberance, no one *wanted* to think of the difference between victory in other countries and victory in Singapore, but differences there were. In the embattled island of Britain, for example, victory had meant freedom from the threat of a tyrant's rule. The war was over and the people of Britain were their own masters again. In the island of Singapore, however, victory had little if anything to do with real freedom. It signalled merely a change in masters – more benevolent than the Japanese, no doubt, but still – masters.

Subconsciously the Chinese in Singapore felt this much more than the other races, for the Japanese had deliberately fostered racial tension during the occupation by singling out the Chinese for torture and death while encouraging the Malays to regard this as their own country and 'sympathising' with the Indians. So the Chinese – the bulk of the population – had more reason

than the other races to remember that the British had
run away, leaving them to the mercy of the Japanese; and
consequently it was mainly the Chinese who wondered
whether the British return might be only temporary.

The mood of euphoria did not last. Buckeridge, who
had lost nearly five stones, was shipped back to England
to recuperate and it was ten months before he was
pronounced fit enough to return to Singapore with Lucy.
In his diary he gives a graphic account of what he found:

Singapore has changed. It is a fortress that has fallen
without a fight, a port without a ship, a city without
people. Some people there are, but they aren't all the
ones we knew. Many of the old faces are here – the
market stall holders, thinner by far, but the few 'men in
the street' seem different. The rickshaws have disappeared, for the Japs had replaced them with trishaws
saying the rickshaw was inhuman. (I think the real
reason was that rickshaw was Chinese whereas the
trishaw was Japanese.) Life has changed. Food is scarce.
Cars are scarce. Petrol is scarce. The only people with
money are the army and its contractors. Army contracts
are the only source of living. Contracts to do work.
Contracts to supply goods. Contracts to supply transport. Contracts to supply labour. Life, it seems, has
become one large 'racket', for none of these items is
available. The only people with money are the services.
The only people with food are the services. The only
people with transport are the services. The only people
with petrol are the services. A *modus operandi* has
developed. The services have everything; the people
want everything. There has been no lack of contact.

The troops who have come to take over the administration are not fighting men, but seem to be composed,
chiefly it seems to me, of those who in the days of the
Japanese invasion, had 'ratted' – had got out. Now here
they are back again in smart uniforms, with badges of
rank, even red tabs. And with them is a crowd of
uniformed underlings who have never lived under the

'British Raj', who never knew of the 'British Empire', whose only instinct is to be 'on the make'. They are billeted in homes undamaged by the Japs. They are looting them. One of them told me his officers had passed the word, 'The place is ours.' They are taking everything they can.

Worst of all was the scandal of food. There was a kind of rationing, but very little to ration. Prices were kept high – and that was rationing enough. Fresh food was virtually non-existent, and for months the returning Europeans lived largely on tinned food. 'But what tins,' Buckeridge recalls. 'They were bent, rusted, decrepit, at astronomical prices. They must have been stolen.'

It was as bad for the locals too, for by 1946 food rationing in Singapore was more stringent than it had ever been in the days of war. The rice ration was reduced to four ounces a day for men, three for women and two for children. Before the war, a man had eaten twelve to sixteen ounces of rice a day. And though the British organised a series of conferences in Singapore on the nutrition problems in South-East Asia, and though China diverted rice to Malaya, it was not enough, and there was a time gap. Rice and flour were not only in short supply on the island, but throughout much of South-East Asia.

At the same time industry, particularly tin and rubber, was hopelessly disorganised. Unemployment was high. There were shortages of textiles, and all these elements exacerbated a crime wave, not only by petty crooks looting and stealing, but by anti-British factions, turning the physical losses into political gain. After all, though the war was over, the widespread humiliation of the white man in Asia made it all too easy for the seeds of another kind of war to germinate; and this time the foe was communism, often thinly disguised as nationalism.

Communism in the Far East had started to take root as far back as 1922, when the Chinese Communist Party opened in Singapore an office of the Nanyang Communist Party (Nanyang being Chinese for South Seas) with a territory including Indonesia, French Indo-China, Malaya as well as Singapore. Recruiting was slow, for prosperity bred indifference to the creed. The party was also an illegal organisation because it had not been registered with the Singapore Government (as all organisations had been required to do since the secret society riots in the nineteenth century). So the party went underground, attempting to infiltrate the trade unions and foment strikes and industrial unrest. In 1930 the Nanyang Party was replaced by the Malayan Communist Party, but though it embarked on a programme of industrial subversion by establishing cells among naval dockyard workers, railwaymen, and in the tin mines and rubber estates, a series of policy turnabouts bewildered the rank and file.

In 1937 Japan attacked China – so Chinese communists and nationalists became allies against the common enemy. Two years later Russia signed a pact with Nazi Germany and the communists were ordered to switch to anti-British and anti-nationalist activities. Then in 1941, Germany attacked Russia and the Party was ordered to co-operate with the British. No wonder the Party made little headway. Then suddenly, with the Second World War and the loss and subsequent liberation of Singapore, the communists became heroes to the people of Singapore, even if self-promoted heroes. As members of the Malayan Peoples' Anti-Japanese Army, they had fought behind the Japanese lines after the white man had surrendered. Their leaders – men like Chin Peng – claimed to have killed or wounded more than two thousand enemy troops, and during the weeks between the Japanese cease-fire and the reoccupation of Singapore and Malaya by British troops, the MPAJA, in their British jungle greens, had taken over effective control of vast areas of Malaya. The guerillas moved into areas evacuated by Japanese, tried and executed many villagers they believed guilty of collaboration.

For a few weeks the Chinese members of Force 136 could boast, with some truth, that they were the only organised body in the country; that they had opposed the Japanese for years without much outside help, apart from that provided by the handful of British officers who led them. Some units remained at large in the countryside. To persuade them to come into the central areas, they were put under the control of local commanders and promised army rations and pay. Every man was given campaign ribbons and a gratuity of about £45.

The situation was ironic. Whatever the misgivings of the British – and they knew the guerillas were hard-core communists – they could hardly fail to pay tribute to dedicated soldiers who had fought so valiantly with men like Spencer Chapman and other British officers. Indeed, the government even arranged for a contingent of MPAJA Chinese to visit London and take part in the victory parade. Chin Peng was decorated with the OBE.

Yet, even as the MPAJA was being disbanded, its troops were hiding huge quantities of arms – some conveniently 'lost' after being parachuted into jungle hide-outs during the war, others seized from Japanese prisoners. This was the one moment in history when, given dynamic leadership, the communists might have been able to stage a coup and possibly take over Malaya and Singapore in the weeks before British troops arrived in force. But that dynamism was lacking – for an incredible reason, unknown to any communists at the time – and the moment passed.

Instead, the soldiers of the MPAJA formed a new army by the simple expedient of changing one word in their name. They now called themselves the MPABA – the Malayan Peoples' Anti-British Army. While the armed soldiers went underground, the rest of the now respectable communists spent the next two years trying to undermine British authority by quasi-legal methods, but with a strange lack of success. The moment was certainly ripe, for communist prestige was high among the Chinese, while British prestige was low. Two communists even served on the Advisory Committee of the British Military Government. Yet all attempts by communists to 'capture' Singapore by working within the constitutional framework failed, as though the communists were haunted by a jinx – as indeed they were.

They tried to work towards power in a number of ways – through sponsoring Chinese schools, infiltrating front organisations like the MPAJA Old Comrades' Association, the New Democratic Youth League, the Malayan Democratic Union and the innocently titled Singapore Women's Association. In the trade unions they recruited new classes of members such as trishaw riders and cabaret girls.

One would have thought that empty bellies would have made for militancy, and the communists did foment one general strike in Singapore in January 1946, but the government reacted quickly, warning that the leaders of strikes called in an attempt to interfere with the processes of law could be deported. The strike fizzled out, despite the fact that communists were still proudly boasting that they had liberated Singapore.

Why did all these attempts fail – at a time when the communists were, to the masses, the real heroes of the day? What jinx prevented them from seizing power, if only partial? The answer lies in a story strange enough, 'impossible' enough to come straight out of a far-fetched work of fiction. The party at the time was split wide open, in itself a not unusual situation. Men like Chin Peng were anxious to flex their muscles, to show their strength, to resort if necessary to violence. Ranged against him was the Secretary-General of the party, Loi Tak, who advocated a more moderate approach, hoping (at least that is what he said) to achieve independence under communism by less violent methods.

This was the situation in 1948 when a bombshell burst inside the party, trapping them into a position from which, if they wanted to survive, they had no alternative but to start open guerilla warfare. Ironically they were forced into the bloody war that lasted twelve years mainly because of the brilliance of a British master spy.

It was a situation which, if it did not change the course of history, undoubtedly accelerated it. Members of the party were becoming increasingly alarmed, critical of their Secretary-General. Though Loi Tak had served the party since pre-war days, and during the Japanese occupation, accusations of 'dictatorship' and 'incompetence' and 'lack of drive' were mounting. Party members openly suggested that the Central Committee was not only incompetent, but was afraid to criticise Loi Tak's 'poor leadership'.

The criticism was embarrassing to many members because Loi Tak had arrived in Singapore before the Second World War with a dazzling reputation. He had, it was said, been sent on the express orders of the Third International. Certainly he had studied communism in Russia and France. He was in fact a Vietnamese and his movements were so secretive as head of the illegal party that few of the members were able to approach him directly. He had, in short, become a legend.

With the changing post-war atmosphere, he seemed (to some members) to be slipping. There was a lack of positive action, and criticism came to a head at a meeting of the Central Committee in February 1947. It was decided to hold another meeting a week later and thrash out, once and for all, the questions of party aims and objectives, and also whether or not the leadership should be changed. On 6 March 1947, 'Central' met as arranged, at a secret rendezvous five miles from Kuala Lumpur. But one man was missing. Loi Tak failed to show up. Even worse for a communist, he had committed the heinous offence of absconding with the party funds. He has never been seen to this day.

To keep up morale, frantic efforts were made to hush up the circumstances of his disappearance, and it was given about that he had been taken ill when suddenly called to Moscow. Whatever party members might have secretly thought, they pretended to understand. It was a vital time to close ranks. Chin Peng, OBE, was nominated as his successor, and he would have been doubly anxious to keep the affair secret had he known the full details of Loi Tak's sudden disappearance.

It was true that Loi Tak had absconded. And it was true that he had been directly responsible for the failure of communism in Singapore and Malaya. But what Chin Peng did *not* know was that the most brilliant leader in Malaya's communist history was no communist. He was a British secret agent who had previously worked in Indo-China until he had been 'blown', whereupon the French had sent him down to the British in Singapore with a note saying, almost in these words, 'This is a very useful chap. You might find him handy.' The British quickly planted Loi Tak in the Singapore Communist Party, and he rose to the top quickly – which meant that for a long time Britain had run the Malayan and Singapore Communist Parties. Loi Tak had only been spirited away, with a new name and passport, when it became clear that his cover was in danger of being blown again.

Not only had Loi Tak kept the British informed of communist activities, but during the Japanese occupation he became, with the connivance of the British, a double agent, working for the Japanese, so was able to provide a direct link between the enemy and Force 136. The communists were manfully trying to keep going under enemy occupation – a difficult problem as they were being systematically betrayed to the Japanese by Loi Tak, notably at one secret meeting which he called on 1 September 1942. The venue was a Chinese squatter settlement near the Batu Caves, a famous landmark a few miles from Kuala Lumpur. More than forty dedicated party leaders arrived for the meeting, but as they waited for Loi Tak at dawn, they were ambushed by Japanese troops. Eighteen were killed, including four political commissars and three regional committee members, most of them from the old guard of the party. Nearly a hundred were taken prisoner. Loi Tak had, of course, tipped off the Japanese.

None of this was known to Chin Peng when he assumed the leadership, and for several months he refused to allow discussion about his predecessor before he had consolidated his own position. But he could not still the rumours forever and he needed that classic recipe for communist failure – a scapegoat to mask the dissension within, the failure of political activity, and above all the increasing criticism of 'high living and dissolute spending' in the local Politburo.

Finally Chin Peng decided to 'tell all' and (though he had no inkling of the real truth) make Loi Tak a scapegoat in order to appease the five thousand armed guerillas of the MPABA training in secret jungle camps. He decided to go further. Because of the internal crisis and the mounting complaints of inactivity by the guerillas, Chin Peng chose deeds rather than words. Irrespective of the fact that Britain had virtually given Malaya a promise of eventual independence, he decided to launch an all-out attack to free Malaya and Singapore from 'the yoke of British imperialism'.

11. War on the Doorstep

In June 1948, the people of Singapore – a Crown Colony for barely two years – woke up to find themselves with a vicious war on their doorstep. The first shots had been fired near Sungei Siput, a straggling township of shophouses, coffee shops, one cinema, typical of the tin mining towns of Northern Malaya. The town was small, surrounded by the pale ochre moonscapes of worked tin mines, the dredging ponds, the lifeless, metallic-coloured water sprouting with tall, straight lilies; and always in the background the grotesque-looking dredges, like half-finished Meccano constructions.

To the east, as the flat country merged into the foothills of the mountain range, the tin mines gave way to rubber plantations, many isolated like the Elphil Estate, which lay twenty miles east of Sungei Siput at the end of one of the loneliest roads in Malaya, a road which only ended when it reached the main office building of Elphil, with its corrugated iron roof, whose manager was Arthur Walker, a man of fifty who had spent twenty years in the country.

Just before eight o'clock on 16 June Mrs Walker drove into town (early to escape the heat) for some last-minute shopping before she and her husband sailed for England and home leave. Like all planters, Arthur Walker made the rounds of the estate before breakfast and shortly after eight o'clock he returned to the office to see his estate clerk, Kumarin, an Indian, and to clear up a few papers. Kumarin went back to his own office which had a window overlooking the main gate.

Shortly before 8.30 three young Chinese rode up to the office on bicycles. Carefully they leaned them up against the building and in no apparent hurry walked towards the door of the office. Walker's dog started barking and he tried to quieten it as the men walked in. Kumarin heard one Chinese say to Walker, '*Tabek, Tuan!*' ('Salutations, sir!'). Walker returned the greeting cheerfully, with apparently no thought that anything was amiss. Within seconds two shots shattered the morning stillness. Through the window, Kumarin saw the three Chinese walk leisurely to their bicycles. For one second, as he peered, terrified, Kumarin's eyes met those of one of the men. The Chinese returned the stare with a cold unsmiling face devoid of emotion. With a touch of arrogance, the man, who seemed to be the leader, stared unblinkingly, obviously to show that he was quite unafraid of being identified by a vital witness. Then, with a gesture that bordered on insolence, he spat once, turned away, and the three men mounted their cycles and calmly rode off down the road.

Kumarin rushed through the communicating door into Walker's office. The estate manager's body lay slumped by the office safe. He had been shot twice, through the heart and chest. The key to the safe lay by his side, and the safe, containing $2000, was untouched.

Within half an hour, and ten miles away, twelve armed Chinese surrounded the main building of Sungei Siput estate; inside, John Allison, the 55-year-old manager, was in his office, while in an adjoining room Ian Christian, his 21-year-old assistant, was discussing the day's work with two Chinese clerks. Christian's office had a separate outside door. Two Chinese with revolvers kicked it open, told Christian and the clerks to put their hands above their heads. As at Elphil, the clerks' most haunting memories are of the cold-blooded, almost casual attitude of the men – 'as though they were soldiers obeying orders and weren't even very interested'.

In English one Chinese coldly asked Christian for his revolver. 'I haven't got one,' Christian replied. No one spoke as the man took a length of cord from his pocket and tied Christian's hands behind his back. As this was happening, three Chinese had burst into Allison's office next door, while the others remained on guard outside. Allison's arms were also pinioned and he too was asked for his revolver. 'It's in the bungalow,' he answered.

The man motioned Allison to stand up. Another man brought in Christian and the two clerks. All were then marched to the bungalow, sited on a rise about a hundred yards distant. With cold efficiency, with no show of emotion, no shouts, no prodding of guns, Allison and Christian were ordered into the bungalow. The two clerks were left outside under guard. Ten minutes later the British were brought out, and were marched to the office. One Chinese turned to the two terrified clerks and reassured them in Malay: 'Don't be afraid. We're only out for Europeans and the running dogs' – 'running dogs' being the communist epithet for British supporters, though later it was used generally for most anti-communists, particularly the police.

As they reached the door, another Chinese motioned with his gun to the clerks to wait outside. Casually he remarked, 'These men will surely die today. We are going to shoot all Europeans.' Within a few minutes, Allison and Christian had been bound in chairs in Allison's office. They were shot sitting in them. The Chinese, completely disregarding the cowed and terrified estate clerks, calmly opened the door, walked out – and disappeared. As at Elphil – as in countless estates in the years to come – no one made any attempt to stop the murders. Only when they were certain the Chinese had gone did one of the clerks telephone the police.

This was the start of a war that lasted twelve years, in which 2473 civilians – mostly planters or miners and their families – were murdered and another 810 were missing. The Security Forces lost 1865 killed, and 2560 wounded. Yet despite the bitterness with which it was fought – and the time it took to beat the communists – it was never given the title of 'war' but was instead always referred to as 'the Emergency' for a peculiar reason. As the author John Gullick, an authority on Malaya and one-time member of the Malayan Civil Service, points out, 'It was a war – though out of regard for the London insurance market, on which the Malayan economy relied for cover, no one ever used the word.' This misnomer continued for twelve years, for the simple reason that insurance rates covered losses of stocks and equipment through riot and civil commotion in an emergency, but not in a civil war.

One supreme irony marked the Emergency. The leaders of the Chinese forces, which numbered about five thousand at the start of hostilities, were all British-trained guerillas who had worked with Spencer Chapman and Force 136 behind enemy lines during the Japanese occupation. They had, during those long years, been quietly hoarding arms. Chin Peng was a remarkable Malayan Chinese aged twenty-six, born in Sitiwan, where his father ran a small bicycle repair-shop. Pleasant-faced, though pimply, he was five feet seven inches tall and walked with a slight limp. He had a quiet, gentle manner, reflected in the soft voice he used to speak six languages, including English. He had joined the Party at eighteen, cutting stencils for the propaganda department, and though some historians believe Chin Peng, who had visited China in 1945 and 1946, was a puppet of Mao Tse-tung, nothing could be further from the truth. This strange, courteous, bookish man was a product of Malayan soil, of his own times, as individualistic as Ho Chi Minh was. Spencer Chapman, fighting the Japanese behind the lines, regarded Chin Peng as 'Britain's most trusted guerilla'.

It had needed a Japanese victory (and subsequent defeat) to promote Malayan communists from a political party into one of organised resistance whose directive had been supplied years previously by the dictum of Lenin: that by the infliction of terror, a well-organised minority can conquer a nation.

The fighting was fearsome, the tortures bloody, the intimidation soul destroying, and those in the front line were the rubber planters and tin miners, for one major objective of the CTs (as the terrorists were known) was to disrupt the economy. And because there was no 'front line' there was a strange air of unreality about the war, a disturbing feeling that nobody in Whitehall was taking it seriously enough; that it was not being prosecuted with enough vigour by the government leaders in London. This indifference in London was reflected among the British and Chinese businessmen in Singapore and Malaya. In the wet, enervating heat that sapped a man's energies, it was only too easy to live the sort of life London had led during the 'phoney war' of 1939; to carry on manfully with one night a week of Home Guard duties, while the *mems* met at tea-parties to roll bandages. Any visitor sipping his *stengah* on the verandah of the 'Spotted Dog' club in Kuala Lumpur would have been hard put to realise that only a few miles out of the city men, women and children were living in conditions of extreme danger.

Only seven miles out of Kuala Lumpur, Peter Lucy, a rubber planter, was under constant attack. During one two-week period in the summer of 1951, there were twenty-five attacks on the Lucy bungalow. On one night alone there were three. The first opened with a fusillade at about eleven in the evening. Peter and his wife 'Tommy' scrambled out of bed, Peter picking up his gun as Tommy ran to bring in their twin baby sons from the nursery. Peter could hear the bullets pinging like hail on the galvanised iron roof. He and Tommy had long since adopted a routine drill to meet the nightly attacks. Tommy manned a Bren gun. Peter dashed outside to lead his Special Constables – not that there was anything positive they could do, for the spurts of flame came from the blackness of the trees and it was quite unthinkable to counter-attack. Yet Peter had to return the fire – for if he did not the CTs would certainly creep up to the bungalow.

This attack lasted twenty minutes, after which they thankfully returned to bed. An hour later it started all over again, lasting for another twenty minutes. And they seemed to have barely dozed off into a troubled sleep before gunfire woke them again at 4 am. After that, Peter had an hour and a half's sleep before he got up to go on his pre-breakfast rounds of the plantation.

Yet the Lucys remained unperturbed. 'Our defences have been improved,' Tommy wrote in a letter. 'We now have two lines of barbed wire round the bungalow area, with two barbed wire gates that are kept locked. We have floodlights at night, eighteen Special Constables on shifts. They are armed with rifles, but we have other weapons about the place; it wouldn't be "security minded" to tell you how many. We won't starve, for the vegetable garden supplies us with spinach for the boys and the dogs, sweet corn, brinjals, radishes, mint and watercress.'

That same week Tommy, whose calm beauty was matched by an equally beautiful figure, did a three-day stint as a model showing off the latest fashions in Kuala Lumpur at a charity bazaar. The Lucys were determined that 'life had to go on'. For, as Tommy wrote: 'If you were sitting with me at the moment, you wouldn't believe I was surrounded by terrorists, that the house is full of guns, that the bar in the living-room is stacked with hand-grenades, and that we might be attacked at any moment. The early mornings in Malaya are astonishingly beautiful; the blue hills are in front of me, bright flowering shrubs and plants in the foreground. The lawnmower sounds very English and the twins are gurgling on the verandah. We try to carry on as if nothing was happening. It's the only answer to our present situation.'

Peter Lucy had one particularly narrow escape when, accompanied by a Malay Special Constable, he was making a routine inspection in a part of the estate which was terraced. Peter carried a twelve-bore shotgun. He looked up, and to his astonishment, 'I saw a bandit in full uniform lying on the ground about twenty yards away. He was facing me and he had a Sten gun pointing straight at me.'

Before the CT could squeeze the trigger, Lucy – using the same technique he had perfected when pheasant shooting in England – twisted round and fired in one swift movement. He shot the man through the head. Almost at the same time the constable saw another uniformed CT ready to fire. He too was shot through the head after which 'two other CTs began firing at us and we decided to retreat'. Lucy's bandit was identified as a local leader called Sin Seng. Peter was awarded the Colonial Police medal and a reward of $2000 which he promptly decided to bank. Tommy had other ideas. 'Oh, no!' she said, 'I hope you'll never have to shoot another CT – so let's have a memento of the occasion.'

As Tommy noted in her diary: 'Finally(!) Peter agreed, and we bought a sapphire and diamond eternity ring (it never leaves my finger) and Peter had a gold cigarette case and studs and cuff-links.'

Obviously every move in Malaya was eagerly watched in Singapore for the whole future of the island depended on the outcome of the hostilities across the causeway. No one can really single out one particular branch of the troops or government and say, 'These were the people who showed the world how communist guerilla warfare can be beaten.' Should that accolade be reserved for men in the hierarchy without whose thinking the war could never have been won? Or for the jungle-bashing troops, the courageous planters, the police? Without any of these the war might have been lost, but these were people who could be seen and known. Behind them, in conditions of the most stringent secrecy, a dedicated band of anonymous men and women played perhaps the single most effective role in eventual victory. This was Special Branch.

No one knew their names or faces. In its simplest form the all-powerful Special Branch can be defined as the internal security department dealing with internal subversion, internal revolution and counter-espionage. It is a little like the British MI5, and bears some similarity to the CIA (though without the latter's wide powers and never setting up external spy networks).

Special Branch agents often operated in Singapore – a natural hiding place for wanted CTs – but their 'think tank' was masterminded in a 'James Bond' special centre hidden behind a rubber plantation on the outskirts of Kuala Lumpur. Here, covering ten acres and surrounded by a ten-foot barbed wire fence, were bugged cells, two-way mirrors, a laboratory for processing documents, a machine shop for work on secret devices, and a nationwide dossier of CTs which was being completed patiently over the years.

In one section Special Branch radio experts were quietly working on scores of ancient battery sets which had been quietly bought up. Each one was taken to pieces, re-made (using only old wire connections and dirtying the solder as anything new would have aroused suspicion), after which each set was quietly 'leaked' to shops known to sympathise with CTs. Special Branch could be sure that sooner or later such a set would reach the jungle – and when it did, when the CT tuned into Peking or Radio Malaya, the set emitted a bleep-bleep homing signal that could not be heard in a jungle camp, but gave precise directions to the nearest British monitoring team.

Intercepted messages played a vital role in Special Branch activities, for it was along the CT jungle courier network that all messages to and from Chin Peng, or between local units and regimental commanders, had to

pass. The courier system was so secret that no jungle post-
man knew more than two 'post offices', but fortunately
Special Branch had several surrendered CT couriers on
its secret payroll who, as double agents, would carry on
normally in the jungle, but on the way from A to B
would lend the documents to Special Branch, who would
photograph them before the CT returned to his normal
duties.

This procedure was not as simple as it sounds, for all
messages were in code and were concealed – sometimes in
fruit, a tube of toothpaste, sometimes in an innocuous-
looking cigarette – and every message had to be returned
looking as though it had not been tampered with – a
particularly difficult task when some CTs started using
invisible ink. Special Branch were able to make this
visible, but this served no purpose for the CTs would
know they were discovered; fortunately Special Branch
scientists discovered a way of making it invisible again.

Special Branch never forgot the success it had enjoyed
over the years when it planted Loi Tak as head of the
Communist Party in Singapore and as the fighting drew
nearer and nearer to the island, the British decided to
repeat the performance in Johore, where a particularly
brutal CT was terrorising the neighbourhood.

The Special Branch man at Kluang in Johore was
called Evan Davies (brother of the late Rupert Davies,
alias 'Inspector Maigret'). Evan had at one time been
Churchill's bodyguard and he was a brilliant operator.
After months of painstaking work he made contact,
through a wife left behind in Kluang, with a 'waverer' in
the jungle camp who visited her from time to time when
fetching supplies of food and medicines.

Because of his long black hair, the CT was known as
'the Raven', and finally he promised to bring out the six
members of his jungle cell, ostensibly on a food gathering
mission. On the day, Davies rose at 3.30 am and led a
patrol of troops together with six Chinese detectives to
the ambush spot on a rubber estate. Communist spies

were so efficient that Davies had to be in position before the tappers arrived – and after reaching the appointed place everyone stood up to their necks in a nearby river to rid themselves of the smell of sweat. No one could smoke, eat or drink. When in position, the last man, armed with a rake, levelled the grass leading to the place where they lay, for the tappers could be working within two or three yards of them.

Shortly after dawn, the Raven appeared, a white scarf tied round his head to identify him, leading a file of six men silhouetted against the grey light. Davies fired. The troops blasted at the rest of the CTs, excluding the one with the white scarf. There was no drama about it – just an exercise in accuracy and speed. Within ten minutes the CT uniforms had been stripped from the corpses and donned by the six Chinese Special Branch men. A few minutes later the Raven was leading them back into the jungle, and the troops were picking up the bodies.

One British soldier was hurt slightly in the leg. And one CT was wounded instead of being killed; and so, after his uniform had been taken, he was dressed in a detective's clothes. Both men were whisked to hospital, where the two enemies were placed side by side in the same ward. They were there, with Davies and an interpreter talking to the CT, when in bustled the ward sister. 'Now then,' Davies remembers her saying fussily, 'you must let these two boys get some sleep. They've obviously had a very busy morning.'

There was a grisly postscript the next day. Special Branch had by now photographic records of virtually every CT, but one of those killed in the ambush was unknown. Two shots through the neck had almost severed his head, and Evan Davies realised that the only man who could identify him was the CT who had been wounded in the ambush and who was now in hospital.

Evan wrapped the head in a brown paper parcel and made his way to the hospital. When he asked the Chinese to identify the head, however, the patient nearly jumped out of bed in terror. Shaking with fear, he explained that all Chinese believed that if they looked on a severed head the spirit of the dead man would haunt them. The persuasive Davies, in his most mellifluous voice, asked, 'Well, if you can't *see* he was beheaded, would that be all right?' The Chinese after some doubts eventually agreed, whereupon the bulky Davies got down on the floor, lay on his back by the bed of the wounded Chinese and lifted the head just far enough for it to be identified but without showing his neck.

Once the head was identified, Davies returned to his office and dumped the parcel on his desk for a few moments. When he returned the door was jammed and only after pressure could he prise it open. Inside on the floor in a faint was Miss Allborough, his secretary. She had opened the parcel imagining it contained papers to file.

Now, of course, Davies controlled a CT cell, and the Raven even had an army radio engineer so that Davies could keep in contact, using an ecclesiastical code. (Davies was referred to as the Bishop, and if they wanted to meet or send messages, the Raven would ask, 'Tell me, Bishop, what hymn shall we be singing at the next service?' Davies would reply with a number indicating a village or map reference.)

Side by side with the cloak and dagger operations was a more hard-headed approach in this strangest of wars: bribery. As the fighting dragged on, as evidence could be seen of Malayan independence, many disgruntled CTs were not averse to giving themselves up, but were often held back by fear. There is, however, one human emotion that is often stronger than fear; that is stupidity. To encourage waverers, the government offered generous 'surrender money' on an arranged basis, so much per head, increasing with rank, which meant that if a CT leader could persuade others to give themselves up, he would 'earn' more.

One communist turncoat who made a fortune by persuading scores of CTs to surrender was Hor Lung, whose Johore camp was close to Singapore. He was vicious, brutal and a proven murderer, but finally he surrendered with so many high-ranking followers that the entire communist operation in Johore was wiped out. Whatever the blood money, it was worth the price. In fact, Hor Lung was eligible for a reward of just over $400,000 – the equivalent of £50,000, causing Tengku Abdul Rahman, the Malayan Prime Minister, to remark, 'He is now richer than any of us.'

Many people hated the idea, and agreed with the *Straits Times* when it asked: 'Are these rewards to terrorist leaders absolutely necessary? Every self-respecting stomach retches at the news.' It was a powerful plea, yet with the war still draining $350,000 a day from the local Federal Treasury (apart from the cost to Britain), who could argue with the reply given by the Tengku when he was asked if he felt it right for Hor Lung to be so richly rewarded?

'We have to get results,' replied the Tengku. 'We cannot stick strongly to principles. If money can buy the end, we must use it.' He paused, then added thoughtfully, 'On principle, of course, Hor Lung should be hanged.'

Long before this – in the middle 1950s – plans for the independence of Malaya (not Singapore, of course) had gathered momentum after a major conference in London agreed to full independence by the end of April 1957. So the major 'objective' of the communists – to get rid of 'the hated British' – no longer applied and this hastened the defections. In the interim period, the Malayan Government would be responsible for finance, internal defence and security. The path of transition to independent statehood had to be trodden warily for Britain was not going to risk a repetition of the French fiasco in Indo-China.

Though the Emergency was at its bloodiest in Johore, north of the causeway, and unspeakable horrors took place only a few miles from Singapore, the fighting never really reached the streets of the island. Of course it impinged on Singapore in many ways. When the British, angry at Chinese support for Malayan communists, ordered an embargo of rubber exports to China, half the mills in Singapore closed, throwing thousands out of work. The loss of production in rubber, tin and pineapples in Malaya brought more unemployment to Singapore, the focal point for all exports. Others were thrown out of work when Air Headquarters Malaya was moved from Singapore to Kuala Lumpur. Many Singapore police were seconded for duties in Malaya, and many died. Members of the Singapore Regiment of the Royal Artillery were killed in action in the peninsula.

The Emergency hastened early independence for Malaya; the British could not afford their usual dawdling discussions because independence became a key factor in victory; it knocked the main plank from under the argumentative feet of the communists. With independence promised, the British could ask waverers, 'What are you fighting for?' And (more important) they could ask innocent people caught up in the war, 'What are you suffering for, with independence round the corner?' Inevitably the speeding up of independence for Malaya provided Singapore with unlimited shot and shell to demand its release from British bondage by becoming part of the soon-to-be-formed Malaysia.

The Emergency also produced one psychological by-product in Singapore that helped in no small way to mould its future stability. The bestiality and ferocity of naked communism in action only a few miles away had a profound effect on Lee Kuan Yew, who was twenty-five when the Emergency started (and a figure of some political stature by the time it ended). There can be little doubt that his intense hatred of communism was nurtured by the Emergency.

12. Enter Lee Kuan Yew

The Emergency had lasted twelve years, and it was during this time that Lee Kuan Yew evolved from a student at Cambridge to a front-rank politician, due mainly of course to his own personality and talents, but also to the blood of his ancestors, who were Hakka Chinese, noted for their arrogance, determination, energy and sense of adventure. The Hakkas hailed originally from northern China, but many had at one stage migrated south to Kwangtung province, and it was from there that Lee Kuan Yew's great-grandfather had originally come to Singapore.

Kuan Yew's father, Lee Chin Koon, determined to educate his son to be the equal of any Briton, and if money was short his wife gave cookery lessons to raise extra funds for the boy's schooling, which began at Telok Kurau English School, where he was known as Harry, a name he continued to use until he entered politics. At twelve he moved to the Raffles Institution, founded by Sir Stamford, and at that time Singapore's most exclusive educational establishment. By 1939, he had won honours and medals and was ready for higher education in England.

The war forced a change of plan, and instead of England, Lee's father had to be content with Raffles College (later the University of Singapore) where the boy read economics, mathematics and English literature and was active in union debates conducted in English. It was also at Raffles that he met Kwa Geok Choo, three years older than him, who had been awarded a scholarship from the Methodist Girls' School.

In 1942 the Japanese came. Lee was nineteen and the Japanese humbling of British power had a deep effect on him. 'They made me and a generation like me determined to work for freedom from servitude and foreign domination,' he said later. But since the Japanese *were* there, he decided to do something practical. He learned Japanese and quickly became a translator for Domei, the Japanese news agency, until 1945, by which time the Japanese defeat seemed inevitable and he fled to the Cameron Highlands in Malaya to wait for the British to return.

After 208 days of British military government. the civilian administration resumed on 1 April 1946   1 in September of the same year, Lee Kuan Yew sailed for England to complete his education, travelling on the troopship *Britannia*, one of only a dozen civilians, all students. Lee landed at bomb-shattered Liverpool and hated it. He spent a term at the London School of Economics and hated that too. 'The idea of rumbling down the tube from Swiss Cottage to Holborn, and dashing round from Holborn to Aldwych ... and getting out to catch I don't know what number of bus to University College ... then back again to King's College ... wasn't my idea of university life,' he wrote later.

After one term Lee moved to the quieter surroundings of Fitzwilliam College, Cambridge, where he read law. Kwa Geok Choo was already at Girton, also reading law (she obtained first class honours in two years). Kuan Yew courted her and they agreed to marry when they returned home.

Lee moved easily into the English way of life and took up golf. More significantly, he joined the Cambridge University Labour Club and the Malayan Forum of Tengku Abdul Rahman, later to be Prime Minister of Malaya and Malaysia, at which plans for a united, independent Malaysia were discussed passionately.

Academically Lee was brilliant. He came first in the honours list with a double first law tripos and a star for special distinction (enabling him to boast later, 'I speak to Harold Macmillan and Duncan Sandys as equals. At Cambridge I got two firsts and a star for distinction; Harold Macmillan didn't'). After being called to the Bar in the Middle Temple, Lee returned to Singapore in 1950, married his childhood sweetheart and after a spell with Laycock and Ong, opened the husband and wife law firm of Lee and Lee, where he leapt into the public eye, first by representing the postal workers' union in a strike, then in 1953 by defending a student journal charged with sedition. He brought D. N. Pritt QC to Singapore to lead for the defence and the charges were quashed.

He became more and more intrigued by politics, specially as he could see that in the newly independent countries of Asia it was the foreign-educated students who had been in the van of liberation movements. In Singapore, the rising tide of nationalism washed all around him; the influence of communism and ethnic groups was already working against the frustrated, weakened white rulers in a colony changed beyond recognition. A man without any false modesty, Lee knew that he was intellectually superior to other young leaders he met; he was also a born orator. Given that knowledge, it was the perfect moment for a brash pragmatist to step into the political bullring. Lee did not step in. He jumped over the *barrera*.

He started as he meant to go on, with no scruples about allying himself with enemies he despised if it suited his purpose, or jettisoning allies if they became tiresome or dangerous. If his aims had been venal or corrupt, his manner of riding roughshod over others would have brought about an early downfall, but even his most virulent enemies cannot deny that Lee's career has always been motivated by a deeply patriotic belief in the future of Singapore.

As a budding politician, Lee's first acts were typical of his approach to a problem. If he wanted to go from meeting to meeting, night after night, to make speech after speech, he needed to be in perfect health. He decided to live a spartan life. He went on a diet. A heavy pipe smoker at Cambridge, he threw his pipes away. He gave up beer drinking – another habit learned at Cambridge. Instead he drank green tea – and unwittingly provided himself with a 'trademark' or symbol; the vacuum flask of tea that he carried with him at every meeting.

With support from trade unions and students, Lee formed his own political party, the People's Action Party, in November 1954, when his supporters on the platform included Tengku Abdul Rahman. This was during the time when the Emergency was at its height. Lee demanded independence for a unified Malaya and Singapore, Malayanisation of the Civil Service, the repeal of emergency regulations imposed by the British, universal adult suffrage and official recognition of the Chinese and Tamil languages.

His sights were set on a new Legislative Assembly to be set up in Singapore under the so-called Rendel Constitution (because it was based on the recommendation of a Commission chaired by Sir George Rendel) which was to give Singapore a large measure of self-government.

The new Legislative Assembly was to be increased to 32 members, 25 of whom would be elected from constituencies. The others would be appointed by the Governor, though he would cease to preside and would be replaced by a Speaker. At the same time the powerful Executive Council would be replaced by a ten-strong Council of Ministers, headed by the Governor, seven of whom would be elected members of the Assembly.

Lee realised that he could not hope to win power in the new Assembly immediately; what he planned was to make PAP the leading opposition party. So he welcomed all leftist support for PAP, including that of communists, and his rallies featured the clenched fist salute.

When the elections were held PAP put up four candidates; three of them, including Lee, were successful. The Labour Front had ten seats and with the support of other minority parties formed a government. It was led by another lawyer, who was also a magnificent orator, none other than David Marshall, the son of the Iraqi-Jewish Saul Nassim Mashaal, who had settled in Singapore as an importer of dates. From the start, Lee was able, as he planned, to establish himself as the voice of opposition. At the very first meeting of the new Assembly he declared in a fiery speech, 'This constitution is colonialism in disguise.'

In a way he was right, for though the English-educated Marshall was an individualist of commanding presence – more like a Shakespearean actor than a politician – he never really worked well with the last of the British, some of whom were at times openly contemptuous of his ancestry and race. They even at first refused to give him a private office and small staff (until he threatened to set up office under a tree). Marshall was liberally minded, a lover of all things British, but was up against a bunch of appalling British dullards, many of them snobs whose petty minds seemed more concerned with enjoying (and prolonging) the dwindling trappings of pseudo-importance before they were booted out to end their drab lives in Cheltenham or Tonbridge. Because of them, Lee Kuan Yew could fire his ammunition on two fronts – against Britain for being obdurate, and against Marshall for being ineffective.

Those who were in Singapore at the time never forgot the magnetic influence of Lee Kuan Yew. George Hammonds, once of the *Malayan Tribune*, but now working for the *Straits Times*, remembers one of his reporters begging him, 'You must come and listen to this man yourself.' George did so – 'and I knew the moment he opened his mouth that he was a spellbinder as an orator – and as a politician.' Lee Kuan Yew and Hammonds met that night and many years later, when George had given up his British naturality to become a citizen of Singapore, Lee Kuan Yew remembered (in a conversation with the author) one of his first 'converts', George Hammonds.

Against the attacks of Lee on the one hand and an eruption of strikes and unrest in unions and schools on the other, Marshall's government lasted only fourteen months before he resigned in frustration after leading an all-party delegation to London to seek independence. Marshall was replaced as Chief Minister by Lim Yew

Hock, but a movement for independence had begun which could not be stopped.

In October 1956 there were serious cases of arson. Students rioted – and PAP members were involved. Of thirty-five communists arrested on security grounds the following year sixteen were PAP members. But by then Lee Kuan Yew was swinging right to avoid appearing a bogeyman to the British, who were nearing the point of agreeing to set up a state of Singapore with full internal self-government. Lee moved communists out of positions of responsibility in PAP, thereby achieving more credibility as a future Chief Minister.

In 1958 Britain conceded defeat. Singapore was to have statehood, with full internal self-government, though Britain would maintain control of defence and foreign policy. New elections would be held in 1959 for a new, enlarged Assembly with a Prime Minister and Cabinet. A Head of State would replace the Governor.

Until then the old Assembly dragged on, graphically described by BBC reporter Anthony Lawrence in his book *Foreign Correspondent* (London, 1972) in which he wrote:

The Government of Lim Yew Hock, with what seems commendable haste, is passing a number of laws designed to please the citizens of Singapore and secure the government's re-election. Measures to provide welfare, arm the police with stronger powers against secret societies, promote public housing ... [but] Parliamentarianism is a faded business here altogether; it bloomed, if it ever did, in another place and long ago. Now the plant crackles like parchment and gives out a dead smell. It is the same in all places of debate when the power has moved elsewhere. In Singapore the power has been moving away from Parliament and Government House, away from the British armed forces GHQ and the Naval Base, out into the noisy streets and alleys of Chinatown. The People's Action Party – Lee Kuan

Yew and his group of fellow politicians – have been organising the masses. Their instruments are the fanatical young ginger groups, the youth leaders and the cadres of the illegal Communist Party.

The time had arrived for Lee Kuan Yew to make his bid for power. In the 1959 elections there were fourteen parties in the field and 190 candidates for the 51 seats. Without a blush, Lee returned to a left-wing revolutionary platform to ensure that the Malayan Communist Party would give the PAP its backing. Britain was so alarmed at the enthusiasm of Chinese communist candidates that they arrested seven communist members of the PAP, and jailed them under security regulations just before the election. On polling day police leave was stopped. Five thousand soldiers, 7000 airmen and 1500 seamen were warned to keep away from the polling areas. But polling, in which many Singaporeans were voting for the first time, passed off quietly.

It was a triumph for Lee Kuan Yew. The PAP received 53.4 per cent of the votes cast. The party had put forward candidates in all 51 constituencies and 43 of them were returned. After the landslide victory, Lee Kuan Yew, Singapore's first Prime Minister designate, told reporters that the verdict of the people had been clear and decisive: 'right had triumphed over wrong, clean over dirty, good over evil'. But he said his party would refuse to take office unless the seven members of PAP in Changi, imprisoned without trial because the British said they were dangerous subversives, were released.

At a news conference later in the City Hall he was more moderate. 'It is simply that, whatever the rights or wrongs of the case, the party has to stand by its members,' he explained, carefully adding a promise that none of the imprisoned men would be in the government. Among the journalists in the City Hall was Anthony Lawrence, who remembers, 'The deep impression he left was of a hard-headed, no-nonsense popular leader, and of a man it would be very dangerous to cross. I never saw anyone so lacking in joviality, so in command of a situation.'

Three days later the jailed members of PAP were released from Changi and met by cheering supporters. Two white doves were uncaged amid salvoes of firecrackers and showers of rose petals.

Meanwhile Lee received a shock. The central executive council of PAP met to choose the Prime Minister and momentarily it appeared that Lee might not be the choice. The mayor of Singapore since 1957 had been Ong Eng Guan, an Australian-educated accountant and a non-communist with a vast popular appeal like that of New York's legendary Mayor La Guardia. After being made mayor he had been arrested for setting off firecrackers in front of the City Hall. He had disdained wigs and robes and chaired meetings in shorts. He had told verbose speakers, 'Shut up'. The public loved him and in the general election he had won his seat with 77 per cent of the vote, the highest vote of any candidate. At the executive council meeting Ong – like Lee – received the votes of half the members. But Lee achieved office by the casting vote of the chairman.

On 3 June 1959 the new State of Singapore came into being and Lee was its first Prime Minister. He was still only thirty-six but a father of three now. His first son, Hsien Loong, had been born in 1952, his daughter Wei Ling in 1954 and a second son, Hsien Yang, in 1955.

13. Freedom through Merger

All history evolves through a series of anomalies, unrelated incidents, quirks of fortune, in much the same way (though on a grander scale) that a man's destiny may change because he takes one fork of a road instead of the other, and so averts a catastrophe of which he will never have any knowledge.

The story of Singapore's fortunes is surely studded with more anomalies than most. Had Raffles not taken the trouble to learn the Malay language, he might have passed the island by and its whole development would have been different. If the British had not stolen rubber seeds in South America and eventually started to grow rubber in Malaya, the prosperity of Singapore would have been different. And in all the ifs and buts two extraordinary anomalies do stand out on the road to Singapore's independence. They take the form, really, of question and answer.

Despite Britain's shrinking empire, she firmly insisted during the post-war years in retaining her strategic strongholds. The Red Chinese might clamour that Hong Kong was Chinese, but with no more avail than the Spaniards bleating that Gibraltar belonged to them. Why then, after the bitter struggle to rid Malaya of communism, and evidence of a more deadly communist onslaught in Vietnam, did Britain tamely relinquish her hold on the most vital strategic base in all South-East Asia?

The answer can only be that Britain was outmanoeuvred by a politician astute enough to realise that an outright demand for the independence of Singapore would be met with an unequivocal refusal. Lee Kuan Yew knew perfectly well that Britain's plans to grant complete independence to Malaya (partly as a means of hastening the end of the Emergency) certainly did not include the Crown Colony of Singapore. To combat this hypothesis, Lee's strategy was masterly, a compound of Western brilliance and Asian patience. Cleverness alone is one thing, but can sometimes be suspect. Sincerity is something else. Lee married the two components of political attack. No one can ever say whether Lee Kuan Yew glimpsed the ultimate goal when he started to walk along the five-year road to independence, but as a passionate believer in the future of his island, with a firm belief that the hardworking Singapore Chinese are infinitely preferable to the more indolent and feudal Malays, who can doubt that from the start he knew where the ploy would end?

Now Lee was elected. He had power – even if portfolios like defence remained in British hands. But Lee determined to use his power with a dynamism and charisma rarely equalled in Asia. Almost overnight Singapore changed from the city of easygoing British *tuans* to a city of galvanic energy. While the last of the British colonialists and businessmen looked on in astonishment, Lee ordered all his ministers to set an example by being at their desks in shirt sleeves at 8 am. Lee himself embarked on a round of talks – with employers and workers, civil servants and students and journalists. He never departed from his theme: Forget separate identities, think of Singapore. Co-operate – or get out.

He warned employers that they would be jailed if they frustrated government policies for industrial peace. He warned newspapers that he would regard them as subversive if they soured moves for closer relations between Singapore and Malaya.

As a first step in creating a more equal society, university academics had their salaries cut and 9000 senior civil servants found their allowances reduced; when they sought to stage a protest meeting Lee banned it. In moves to curb bureaucracy, the civil servants were instructed to be more civil and the public was invited to report cases of rudeness by people like post office clerks. At the same time he launched an almost puritanical drive against corruption, and against 'yellow culture' – Western girlie magazines, strip shows, juke boxes.

In 1960 Lee's leadership was challenged by Ong who had become Minister for National Development, and also treasurer of PAP. Ong's constituency party put forward sixteen resolutions ostensibly designed to make PAP more democratic but, with communist support, Lee turned the party meeting into a trial of Ong; the former mayor and two supporters were expelled from the party and his branch committee was suspended. But Ong still enjoyed enormous popularity; at a by-election which followed Ong trounced the official PAP candidate, Jek Yuen Thong, a Chinese left-winger, obtaining 75 per cent of the popular vote.

It was a setback for Lee, who reacted by learning Hokkien, which was Ong's dialect, and Mandarin in a bid to win greater Chinese support. In fact, Ong's challenge was to peter out over the years.

By this time Lee's main concern was a merger with Malaya. He had declared immediately after the 1959 general election that internal self-government was but a step towards complete independence and by becoming (as he hoped) part of independent Malaya, he would at least be independent of Britain. His slogan became, 'Freedom through merger'.

Lee held that the two went together. Britain would never allow Singapore full independence in isolation because of the island's preponderance of Chinese to Malays – the reverse of the division in Malaya which had achieved independence in 1957, during the Emergency. Britain feared that if Singapore were granted full independence it would fall to the communists and cause security problems.

Lee knew that his tactics were right, but even so the merger question was explosive. The communists in Singapore demanded independence for Singapore immediately, with no strings attached – partly because they feared that a merger would bring about their suppression by the Malays. Meanwhile in Malaya, the people were cool towards a merger. Their state of emergency had ended officially only in 1960 and having succeeded in defeating their own communists they were not interested in tackling Singapore's.

But both Lee and Tengku Abdul Rahman, now Malaya's Prime Minister, were still convinced of the merits of merger, the cause which they had espoused in England when Lee was still a student. In July 1961, after a conference between Singapore, Malaya, North Borneo, Brunei and Sarawak had declared in favour of merger,

Lee and Rahman signed a pact and Britain was left with no alternative but to accept the plan, subject to retaining its bases in Singapore.

Almost immediately Lee was faced with a dramatic – and nearly disastrous – split with his left-wing supporters. They claimed Lee was moving to the right again, maintaining Singapore as a capitalist society. The merger pact brought differences to a head, and the left wing of the PAP resigned, forming a new party, the Barisan Sosialis, under Lim Chin Siong, one of the seven communists who had been jailed by the British at the time of the 1959 general election. It was estimated that nearly three-quarters of PAP's membership deserted to the new party; whole branches changed allegiance.

Now Lee had only the remnants of a party; but he did have the government, together with support from the United Malay National Organisation and the Singapore People's Alliance, which helped him to retain an overall majority in the Assembly. The Barisan awaited the next general election, due in 1964, confident that they would then win power.

Lee outmanoeuvred them. Firstly, he called a referendum on the merger. It had been agreed with Britain that the Federation of Malaysia should be formed in August 1963. Lee fixed 1 September 1962 for the referendum. In fact the referendum was so skilfully worded that it offered no opportunity to vote on the *desirability* of a merger, only on the *terms* of a merger. Nor was there much choice about terms: voters could opt only for merger on terms set out in a Singapore Government White Paper or on two variations which were insignificantly different. Voting was mandatory. When the Barisan urged voters to return blank papers the government announced that blank papers would be counted as votes for the government plan.

In the event 144,077 returned blank papers but there were 417,482 marked votes of which 397,626 favoured the White Paper proposals. This was a 71 per cent majority for the government plan under which Singapore ceded control over foreign policy, defence and security (which it had never enjoyed anyway) to a central Malaysian government in Kuala Lumpur. It retained power over finance, industry and education, and would keep 60 per cent of its revenue. It would have 15 out of 159 seats in the federal legislature and keep its own parliamentary assembly and head of state. It was envisaged that a common market and customs union would follow.

Lee then promptly sent more than a hundred outspoken critics of the merger proposals into jail. On the radio, three days after the referendum, he explained: 'Before 1 September, firmness would have been misrepresented as fascist oppression. After 1 September I am sure you will want me to do what is right for the security and well-being of all in Singapore and Malaysia.'

He then turned his attention to the Barisan, bringing forward the general election to September 1963, to follow the formation of Malaysia, which was scheduled for 31 August. The election amounted virtually to a straight fight between the PAP and the Barisan. Lee ordered that official campaigning should be limited to the constitutional minimum of nine days, and since during those nine days there were to be festivities to mark the birth of Malaysia, the campaign period was effectively halved. The Barisan had little chance to make an impact on the electors. Meanwhile in November 1962 Lee began a Prime Ministerial tour of all 51 constituencies, ostensibly 'to ensure the performance of the Singapore government is kept up to the best possible level of achievement.' And in February 1963 the government launched Operation Cold Store. One hundred opposition leaders were rounded up and jailed, among them Barisan chiefs including Lim Chin Siong.

As the elections drew near, opposition parties claimed that they had difficulty in getting literature printed because all the printers had been swamped with government work, while the PAP election addresses had been printed months previously in Hong Kong. Barisan unions complained that their bank accounts were frozen by the Registrar of Trade Unions.

In the event the PAP received 46.9 per cent of the popular vote which gave it 37 of the 51 seats; the Barisan had only 13 seats. So Lee Kuan Yew's men went to Kuala Lumpur to join the Malaysian Federal Parliament. Opposition to the merger did not end, however, when Malaysia came into being. Apart from strikes and student demonstrations in Singapore, the formation of Malaysia brought another charismatic – though very different – personality on to the stage; one whose delusions of grandeur helped Lee to attain his ultimate aim. He was none other than Achmad Sukarno, the bombastic, dictatorial president of Indonesia, who had been a critic of federation plans from the beginning. He objected to an imperial power disposing of its possessions without his agreement as head of the major power in the area, and he feared an encircling movement against his country. He had infiltrated his first guerillas into Malaysian Borneo early in 1963.

At a rally in July 1963 he expressed his determination to crush Malaysia – 'a British project aimed at destroying the Indonesian revolution'. Later he declared a policy of 'confrontation' with Malaysia. The exact nature or meaning of 'confrontation' was not spelt out – though the actions were, starting with the burning and sacking of the British Embassy in Jakarta in September 1963. The calm marching and bagpipe-playing of Major Roderick Walker, the British assistant military attaché, only exacerbated anti-British, anti-Malaysian feelings. British cars were set on fire, British homes looted and British businesses seized. Economic sanctions against Malaysia were imposed. Shipments of Indonesian oil and natural gas were banned and it was made an offence, punishable by a year's jail, for Indonesians to listen to Malaysian radio.

Soon Indonesian soldiers crossed the 970-mile-long jungle frontier between Indonesia and Malaysian Borneo into Sarawak and Sabah, ostensibly 'to liberate Malaysian Borneo from the neo-colonists'. Fighting broke out.

Malaysia called up reservists to be sent to Sarawak and Sabah, and Duncan Sandys, Britain's Colonial Secretary, who happened to be in Kuala Lumpur for the Malaysian celebrations, promised that Britain would help to defend Malaysia.

The threat however was not only in Borneo. An Indonesian sabotage base with military training facilities was discovered on Palau Sakupang in the Rhio archipelago, close to Singapore. The commander, Lieutenant Bambang Partono, was a former Indonesian naval attaché in Singapore. He controlled a network of agents briefed to blow up the water mains between Singapore and Johore and to sabotage road and rail communications. Thirty-seven people were arrested in Singapore, Johore, Kelantan and Selangor. Sten guns, grenades and other arms were seized. Within the next few months, another 89 people were arrested in Malaya and 60 in Singapore, all of them alleged Indonesian spies or agents.

By this time vigilante groups had been established in Singapore and elsewhere to help security forces guard public installations and to report the presence of strangers, particularly in coastal villages. Even so, in the summer of 1964 there was rioting between Malays and Chinese in Singapore which was officially ascribed to Indonesian instigation.

In the first riot, in July, 22 died and 500 were injured; more than 200 were arrested. Tengku Abdul Rahman said he had evidence that the Indonesians were behind the riots. In a second spell of rioting, in September, another 13 died, 78 were injured and 700 were arrested. There was proof that Indonesia had paid powerful Chinese gangsters in Singapore's secret societies to keep up the pressure on the authorities.

Meanwhile real warfare moved nearer to Singapore. In August 1964 a force of 100 Indonesians landed on swampy coastland in Johore, 50 miles north-west of the island. In November a smaller force landed on the Kota Tinggi area of Johore, 50 miles north-east of Singapore. In both cases they were mopped up. Then a sabotage group was intercepted off Singapore by a Malaysian patrol boat, and in December 9 Indonesians, heavily armed though not in uniform, were caught two days after being landed on the west coast of Singapore Island. In January 1965 another 24 were landed in the same area from a fast Indonesian assault craft.

The 'confrontation' only ended after Sukarno became a sick man, receiving acupuncture treatment. In March 1966 an army group led a coup in Indonesia which stripped him of much of his authority and began his gradual eclipse. (He was deposed in 1967 and died in 1970.)

In the curious way that a political wind invariably does *someone* some good, Indonesia's prolonged attack on Malaysia made it much easier for Lee Kuan Yew to move towards his real goal – complete independence. Singapore was now entirely free of British domination (except for a treaty concerning bases) and therefore, as Lee Kuan Yew argued, if he severed ties with Kuala Lumpur, Singapore would become a separate country and there was nothing Britain could do about it. There were many in Britain who did not take the possibilities seriously for one simple reason – how on earth, they asked, could a tiny island like Singapore, filled with Chinese coolies, possibly hope to exist by itself? The idea was ridiculous!

It did not worry Lee Kuan Yew. The 'confrontation' had conveniently started a rift between Lee and his Malayan opposite numbers. Lee became increasingly critical of the federation which he had done as much as anyone to bring about. He criticised its policies on finance and represented it as ultra-conservative, compared to progressive Singapore. He irritated the Malays particularly by voicing his criticisms abroad during visits to other countries where his fluency made him Singapore's finest ambassador.

The Malays charged that in a federation of equals, Singapore regarded itself as more equal than the others, and became alarmed at the way in which Lee's men sought to dominate the Malaysian Federal Parliament. What really infuriated the Malay leaders was that while other Prime Ministers had given up their titles and had become simply Chief Ministers of their countries, Lee alone retained the title Prime Minister. Tengku Abdul Rahman, Prime Minister of the Federation, complained: 'There can never be two Prime Ministers in one nation.' Lee, with his prestige increasing internationally, ignored the complaints.

A suggestion was made that Lee should be sent to the United Nations as Malaysian Ambassador. Lee said he was willing – for a short period – but the Malays feared that this might give him an even better platform, so the proposal was dropped. Instead, some critics even began to press Tengku Abdul Rahman to have him arrested.

In May 1965 Lee precipitated the end of federation by staging at his official residence a Malaysian Solidarity Convention, with the avowed object of 'organising a loyal united opposition to fight external aggression and internal dissension'. In fact, though it was attended by delegates from the Malay peninsula and Sarawak, in reality it was a PAP platform and it exacerbated the rift. Malaysian Finance Minister Tan Siew Sen said PAP were shouting 'Fire!' while committing arson. Home Minister Dato Ismail compared Lee to Jekyll and Hyde in the way he spoke abroad and acted at home. Deputy Premier Tun Razak said, 'If the people of Singapore wish to maintain this relationship with us they must find another leader who is sincere. Mr Lee does not care what happens to the people as long as he can get into power.'

At the time Tengku Abdul Rahman was ill in a London clinic, but while convalescing he finally decided that Singapore must leave the federation. He had a Bill drafted to bring this into effect by the time he returned to Malaysia.

On Sunday, 1 August, Lee took his family to the Cameron Highlands on holiday. On Friday one of his ministers telephoned him to say he was needed in Kuala Lumpur urgently; the Tengku was asking Singapore to withdraw. Lee reached the Malaysian capital that night. The next day, after a meeting with the Tengku, he agreed on the separation.

The news broke the following Monday when the Bill came before the Federal Parliament; by that time Lee and his colleagues were back in Singapore. The Tengku told the House there were only two courses open: to take repressive measures or to sever all connections with the Singapore Government which, he said, had 'ceased to give even a measure of loyalty to the central government.' The Bill was passed and became the Constitution of Malaysia (Singapore Amendment) Act of 1965. After less than two years the merger was dead.

Both the Tengku and Lee expressed official regret at the separation. The Tengku charged that Singapore had refused to co-operate in contributing to the national economy, in meeting its share of expenditure on defence and security, and in integrating its port into the national economy. He also complained about the status accorded to Lee.

There has been certain inclination on the part of some countries to look upon the Prime Minister of Singapore as an equal partner in the government of Malaysia and to encourage him directly to assert his authority, and this has made the situation rather awkward for us. This is the situation we must avoid. There can only be one Prime Minister for the nation, and so the best course we can take is to allow Lee Kuan Yew to be the Prime Minister of independent Singapore in the full sense of the word, which otherwise he would not be.

Lee appeared on television, describing the separation as a moment of anguish for him, because he had spent all his adult years working for the unity of Singapore and Malaya. Then he wept and a press conference was postponed for fifteen minutes while he recovered.

'I don't know why Mr Lee acted like that,' observed

the Tengku cynically. 'He was quite pleased about it.'

Then Lee made a speech claiming that a progressive Singapore had been held back by its less advanced partners. 'If they think they can squat on a people, they have made the gravest mistake of their lives,' he said:

> I know why they are doing this ... they want to slow down our pace so that their society – a mediaeval feudal society – can survive. Because if we surge forward at the rate we have been doing, in five or ten years there would have been an even greater disparity and contrast between an effective open society and a closed traditional society. Here, if you want to stand up or if you don't want to stand up, that is your business, but nobody crawls .... What hurts them is fear. It is not so much envy as fear.

The Malaysian Government sent a formal note of protest about this speech and Singapore retaliated with a note of protest about reports of a speech by the Chief Minister of Sarawak.

Britain had not been officially warned of the break-up. As Lee argued, this was really an internal family quarrel, and as such, was no concern of an outsider – in other words, of Britain. But Britain did have a High Commissioner, Viscount Head, who not unnaturally became thoroughly alarmed and immediately telephoned Lee Kuan Yew to arrange an urgent meeting. He was told that Lee was 'unavailable'. Head continued to try and arrange a meeting, and finally Lee agreed to meet him late one night. The details of Lord Head's discomfiture were vividly reported by T. J. S. George in *Lee Kuan Yew's Singapore* in which he wrote:

> What happened was described by Lee himself to a group of British correspondents. 'The first question I asked him [Head] was, "Who are you talking on behalf of?" And he [Head] said, "Well of course, you know I am accredited to a foreign government?" I said,

"Exactly. And have you got specific authority to speak to me about Singapore's relations with Britain?" He said, "No." I said, "Well then, this is a tête-à-tête." He said, "Well, if you like to put it that way." And it *was* that way. And he took it very nicely. He is a toughie, you know; a brigadier in the army, former defence minister ... But ... he knew exactly where I stood. He knew it was not the time of day or the part of the world to do a Cuba: the Bay of Pigs was not possible in Singapore. Or the whole thing would have come crashing down. And I said to him: "You know of course, as far as I am concerned, I will prefer my first recognition from an Asian country such as India. And if I were you, I would get in touch with the British High Commissioner in India, Mr John Freeman, of whom I happen to be a friend, and tell the Indian government that the British really cannot intervene. Once the British say that, the Indians will recognise me." He did not do that. He whipped back to Kuala Lumpur. I do not know what signal he sent to London, but within seventeen hours I got recognition from the British government.'

Lee emphasised the new independence of Singapore by one other tough quote. When he was asked what would happen if the British withdrew their bases, and if he would ask for American aid, he warned the Americans, 'You are not dealing with Ngo Dinh Diem or Syngman Rhee. You do not buy and sell this government ...'

So at forty-two, Lee Kuan Yew became Prime Minister of a fully independent Singapore. In December 1965 legislation was passed (retrospective to 9 August) creating it a republic. Singapore became a member of the British Commonwealth of Nations and of the United Nations. Independence had indeed come through merger.

Part Four

An Experiment in Living (1965-78)

14. The Multi-racial Society

Singapore was an instant success from the moment the British – in the person of Stamford Raffles – landed on its shores. It has, if possible, been an even bigger success since the day the British left and Lee Kuan Yew took over. It is a success achieved despite tremendous odds stacked against it. The island has no resources – no food, no space, no raw materials – nothing but people; two and a quarter million people to be fed and housed. Yet the inhabitants of today's Singapore have taken part in an economic miracle that has staggered the world. They enjoy the highest per capita income in Asia after Japan; their economic growth is the envy of many a western nation; the city has become the world's fourth largest port; it has largely replaced Hong Kong as the financial centre of Asia; the country has no unemployment. In addition it has escaped many of the trials and tribulations that beset more 'advanced' countries. It is unsullied by corruption; it has little or no drug problem, its crime decreases year by year. Half the population lives in government flats, and the island state does not even suffer from that most dreaded of all plagues in emerging nations, a population explosion.

How has it been achieved? As Professor John Kenneth Galbraith pointed out in *The Age of Uncertainty* (London, 1977), it is all too glib to suggest that Singapore's success rests on its geographical position at the crossroads of East and West. Suez and Panama – particularly the latter – are also vital junctions between continents, but they do not enjoy the same prosperity as Singapore. One has to look further, and examine the stability of Singapore's remarkable multi-racial society.

Chinese, Malays, Indians *work* in Singapore – far harder than they ever worked under the British Raj, not only because the wages are good, the housing better than before, the opportunities for their children more hopeful, but because their lives lack the element of tension that exists in the lands of their fathers.

The average Chinese in Singapore earns six times as much as his brother in Communist China – and has no reason to flirt with communism because if he wants to be a communist, he can take the next plane to China. The average Indian in Singapore earns nine times as much as his impoverished brother in India, and suffers from none of the repressions his brothers have suffered during the tyrannical rule of some Indian leaders. Today – under a ruler who certainly clenches an iron fist inside his velvet glove – the mixture of three races has produced a remarkable and basically unfettered polyglot cohesive force. In a masterly analysis, quoted in part, Professor Galbraith, puts it this way:

> I would attribute much in Singapore to the excellent ethnic mixture. The mandarins are the Chinese; they bring to Singapore their art and their ancient experience of organisation. Singapore is organised – led – by the Chinese; Malays provide the traditional crafts, and services; and Indians are traders, lawyers, in the professions ... And there is Lee Kuan Yew, the all-purpose politician. He is one of the more remarkable and durable people of our time ...
>
> The Singapore Government makes pragmatic use of all ideas and refuses to be the captive of any one idea. There can be few places in the world where self-interest is pursued more diligently and with more visible enjoyment in the results.
>
> Public and private outlays are related, as a matter of course, to the availability of workers and the current and the prospective capacity of the economy. When other people talk of an incomes policy, Singapore economists and businessmen and union leaders must

surely yawn, because they have had one for many years.

Is there planning, is there socialism in Singapore? The answer again, is yes. If housing, the harbour works, transportation, trained people (many of these are needed) or other things are required, the government provides them. Self-interest serves pretty well as a motivation, but it is recognised in Singapore that it does not serve all purposes, and that it serves best within a framework of careful overall planning ...

Singapore does provide its people with a decent and very agreeable existence.

Behind this success story is the man who has wielded almost absolute power since the day Singapore became a republic – and who provides the living lie to the saying that power corrupts. Lee is the only living politician in Asia against whom no one, not even his bitterest enemies, has been able to hurl accusations of corruption. His life has never been touched by scandal. His dedication is almost frightening. His only hobby is golf. He is a non-smoker, non-drinker, he never reads a book for pleasure, never listens to music, never looks at a movie. Every morning he exercises to make sure that his weight never varies; he eats virtually no breakfast, often no lunch, and only a light evening meal. He never touches bread or rice.

Above everything else is his almost terrifying single-ness of purpose. From his air-conditioned office in the old Government House (always kept at 72 degrees) he started from the first day to direct almost every facet of Singapore's life.

When Singapore became a republic, his first task was to turn a city into a country. There were examples for him in Europe, such as Monaco and Liechtenstein (which were smaller) and Luxembourg (which was bigger). Geography helped him, as it had helped Raffles, but it was work, industry, that turned the scales.

From being the biggest warehouse in Asia, Singapore became South-East Asia's biggest workshop. A start had already been made. With the aim of serving Malaysia, an

Economic Development Board had been established in 1961 and in the years that followed, the government channelled millions into expanding power and water supplies, building roads and clearing factory sites. Electronics, metal fabrication, optical instruments and diesel engine plants were set up. By 1964 manufacturing had outstripped the historic *entrepot* trade, accounting for 12 per cent of the gross domestic product, compared to 10 per cent from *entrepot* trade. The value of goods and services produced in Singapore doubled between 1959 and 1969.

School leavers were pressured to become engineers and technicians rather than clerks and shop assistants. Taiwan and South Korea offered cheaper labour but Singapore's workforce had advantages such as familiarity with the English language, and the island's port was unrivalled except by Hong Kong. By 1967 the port of Singapore was handling more shipping than London.

Seventy-five per cent of its cargo was oil, for Singapore became oil-rich without actually producing any. Four modern refineries process crude oil from the Persian Gulf for shipment to Japan and Australia.

There were, of course, hiccups in the republic's smooth progress. In 1965, the first year of full independence, the factories fell on hard times and rising unemployment brought fears of a communist power bid.

Lee, who knew that Singapore could never survive with British trade union practices, had already acted against militant union leaders, arresting the noisiest of them and banning the Singapore Trade Union Congress in 1963. He substituted a National Trade Union Congress with hand-picked leaders in its place. In 1968 an Industrial Relations Ordnance and an Employment Act made arbitration in any dispute compulsory, backed management powers to hire and fire, curtailed the right to strike, increased working hours and reduced sickness and retirement benefits.

To boost local exports, Lee sent trade delegations all over the world, while Singapore's loveliest girls were entered in world-wide beauty contests to boost the tourist trade which brings a million visitors a year and helps to support factories turning out souvenirs like umbrellas and clogs and a whole range of products bearing the images of Raffles or trishaws ...

As the republic moved ahead, Lee never lost sight of the fact that all would collapse unless he ruthlessly dealt with any pro-communist threats. To do this two unique priorities emerged: to lock up any dangerous left-wing agitators and then to produce a truly multi-racial society with a standard of living high enough to make any communist overtures uninteresting to the average Singaporean. Of course Lee has invited bitter criticism for his 'oppressive form of government', mostly (but not always) from those who howl with rage at the mention of Chile's repressive regime, but who beam with delight when welcoming Soviet murderers to the shores of England.

Since this story spans more than a hundred and fifty years (of which Lee is concerned with only a few) it is not intended to become a political forum. However, it must be said that if it is undesirable to lock up political opponents without trial, as it certainly is, life must be equally unpleasant for the political opponents who still manage to exist in the city that was once called Saigon, or for the Jews who only ask to leave an oppressive regime in Russia and are denied the opportunity to start new lives elsewhere. Whatever the faults that may be laid at Lee's door, no one can accuse him of forcing people to live in Singapore if they do not want to. There are no exit visas. Anyone can leave without a fuss. Lee may have evolved a form of government that is not to everyone's liking, but those who do not like it are free to go elsewhere – and take their money with them. It is as simple as that.

Above all Lee is a realist. When he was asked (during an interview in 1977) how he could justify keeping people in jail for years without trial, he gave a simple answer. All any detainee has to do, he said, is to say (not even write) the following sentence in public, 'I denounce the use of force. I do not support the Malayan Communist Party in their use of force to overthrow the government.'

'But,' added Lee, 'if they believe as I think they do, that there will, one day, be a great victory parade, and they will be on the rostrum, where all the local Lenins and Maos will be, well, then they stand firm on principle, and wait for tomorrow.' And he added these significant words in answer to a question on television:

> I am also a realist. The magnitude of what one terms licence, or civil liberties, or personal freedom, has got to be adjusted to the circumstances. And, as far as the communists are concerned, they want it both ways: both the ballot and the bullet. They want the ballot, and the processes that go before the ballot to aid them, both internally and internationally, in the use of the bullet. They learnt it from the Vietnamese: the battle was not fought in Washington, it was fought in the streets of Stockholm, it was fought in Sydney, in Melbourne, in Paris, in London.
>
> Now, they are trying to do to me – which they must try – and they are trying to do to all the other non-communist governments in the region, what they did to Thieu. If they can portray me as corrupt, fascist, dictatorial, capricious, wicked, vicious, then half the battle is won.

Lee needs educated anti-communists, so there are no reds under the dormitory beds of Singapore's 541 schools – or under the teachers' beds either. Elitism is the keystone of Singapore's education system – élitism to help create the wealth and administrative ability which the tiny republic needs, plus bilingualism to act as the cement in its multi-racial society. Streaming begins on a child's first day at school when it is assessed on 'bio-data' based on family background and home environment, pre-school education and aptitude. This tends to group children of the same socio-economic background together. The streaming continues throughout school life.

For those with ability there is university education – providing the student wins a suitable certificate from the Ministry of Education in a screening process designed to bar 'undesirable' elements from higher education and prevent political unrest in the universities. (At the first sign of trouble, Lee dissolved the students' union at the University of Singapore.) Those who fail to make the higher streams are diverted into streams leading to apprenticeships for manual work, for Singapore still needs skilled labour. The bilingualism policy requires each child to be proficient in its mother tongue and in one other language, which is most frequently English. (The official languages of the island are Chinese, Tamil and Malay.)

Lee's dictum is simple: you go to school to learn. Nobody forces you to go, but for those who hope to become élitist leaders education is a privilege. It costs nothing, and everyone has an equal chance to continue his education. But since it is free, Lee argues that a student owes it to society to repay the debt with hard work and good manners. As one Singaporean put it, 'Nobody forces a boy to go to school. If he doesn't like the system, he doesn't have to take it. He can always become a trishaw coolie.'

One can appreciate the argument that rebel youth has historically always been in the van of change – and no one provides a better illustration of this than Lee himself – but his basic concept is that above all Singapore needs stability as it builds for the future. And the interesting factor of his somewhat draconian education system lies in the results: while many countries wallow in an educational quicksand, Singapore, according to a UNESCO report, has the highest literacy rate in South-East Asia, and its newspaper and book readership are the highest in the area.

Lee's toughness spills over into many social areas, and it is intriguing to note how they are all interconnected, not only by a violent hatred (and fear) of communism, but by a deep-rooted belief that cleanliness is next to Lee-type Godliness, or that crime must never be allowed to pay because once lawlessness takes over, anarchists find it easier to operate.

Singapore itself shines like an advertisement for a new kind of furniture polish. It is almost too good to be true, but why should critics jeer at what one called 'the anti-septic society of Singapore'? Most of Asia is a pigsty of filth, largely through ignorance and lack of training or just plain apathy. In the midst of Asia stands Singapore, so spotless that London by comparison is filthy and New York looks like an unemptied dustbin.

Lee himself has almost a fetish for cleanliness. His nails are always carefully trimmed, he washes his hands several times a day, he changes his shirts and vests twice a day or more frequently. Even his shoes are dazzlingly polished. He argues that cleanliness in public places helps uneducated people to appreciate cleanliness (and consequently hygiene) in public places. If you slap a fine of $100 on anyone who discards litter on the streets, one gets into the habit of not throwing litter anywhere. Compare the beaches at Changi with those of an English coastal resort.

Lee faced similar snide remarks when he outlawed long hair for males. For the minority, who keep their long hair regularly washed and waved and set (at considerably more expense than their girl friends) long hair may do no harm. But dirty, unkempt long hair *does* do harm, as was proved when the West German army finally bowed to public opinion and allowed drafted soldiers to retain their long hair: the incidence of lice and nits among soldiers rose to 60 per cent. There is a resident hairdresser at Singapore airport to chop off any offending locks, though the rule against long hair has been relaxed (probably partly because of tourists). However, a man with long hair always gets served last in a post office or other government building where he needs help.

Lee is even more ruthless with drug pushers – as he is with all crime. In countries like Britain and America, in

Italy and France, crime increases because crime pays. When some drug-crazy child molester and murderer is caught, there are always do-gooders concerned with 'rehabilitating' the poor fellow so that he can re-enter society – and carve up another little girl. Not so in Singapore. Six men were hanged in 1976 for drug trafficking (the death penalty is invoked in drug cases where the quantity involved exceeds a given amount). Six were hanged for murder, three for armed robbery. That was the year – 1976 – when Singapore's crime rate, which has been steadily decreasing under tough measures, was the lowest for nineteen years; at a time when the crime rate in every Western society is increasing at an alarming rate.

Inevitably there was some bitterness between Singapore and Malaysia for several years after the island withdrew from the Federation. It was marked by a series of petty squabbles – like the occasion in 1966 when the Singapore Regiment returned from service in Borneo and was unable to get into its old barracks on the island because they were occupied by a battalion of the Royal Malay Regiment. For some time the Malay Regiment stood on an agreement made during the merger and refused to move out. Singapore began to charge school fees for non-residents attending schools on the island; Malaysia announced that Singapore (which handled 40 per cent of Malaysia's external trade) would cease to be the major centre for its imports and exports. The common immigration control system was ended and separate currencies were introduced in 1967.

But by 1970 rapprochement was near and Lee Kuan Yew was due to make a two-day goodwill visit to Kuala Lumpur for the first official contact between the Singapore and Malaysian heads of government since 1965. It did not take place. Three Malaysian youths detained by the Singapore police had their long hair trimmed, and this aroused so much ill feeling that Lee's visit was cancelled.

It did finally take place in 1972, seven years after the end of the merger, but even then relations were strained for a new quarrel had broken out. It centred on the winding-up of Malaysia-Singapore Airlines. Singapore planned to cash in on the goodwill value of the familiar initials MSA by calling its new independent line Mercury Singapore Airlines. The Malaysians were furious at this piece of commercial acumen and threatened litigation. Eventually Singapore conceded and created Singapore International Airlines while Malaysia formed its Malaysian Airline System. Lee's attempt to use MSA for Singapore's airline is typical of his personality. One of his problems is that he bubbles with new ideas, and if one engages his attention, he follows it through to the end, however unimportant it may be. He lost out with MSA, but some of his ideas pay unexpected dividends.

When the peak hour traffic problem in downtown Singapore – around Collyer Quay and Raffles Place – became 'insoluble', he solved it by imposing a 'fine' of £1 for every car driving into the area during specified rush hours unless it contained four passengers. The result was staggering – for neighbours took it in turns to drive each other to work, resulting in a three-fold bonus – improved neighbour relations, a saving in petrol, and a marked easing of the traffic problem.

This was a minor problem, but all that Lee and his government have tried to do over the years would have been valueless had the people not been housed, fed, and given worthwhile jobs to do. Today Singapore has no unemployment. How this came about is the story really of Lee's pragmatic ability to make bricks without straw, and to turn one disaster into success.

15. Breach of Promise

In January 1968, less than three years after Singapore had achieved full independence – and while Lee was still struggling to build a thriving city-state of two million people on an island lacking all raw materials – Britain dealt its new partner in the Commonwealth the kind of below-the-belt body blow usually reserved for asset strippers or dubious financiers unconcerned with the fates of their friends, let alone their enemies.

For Harold Wilson, Prime Minister at the time, decided to strip Singapore of one of its most precious assets – guaranteed employment for several years. Despite firm pledges to maintain British bases in Singapore until the mid 1970s, he told the House of Commons that all troops would be phased out as an economy measure, the last men to be withdrawn by the end of 1971.

At the same time he announced that a British military presence *would* be maintained in Hong Kong. From the military point of view the decision seemed absurd. British troops in Hong Kong could never hope to combat communist aggression – the only possible aggression in South East Asia at the time – from an isolated, waterless chunk of rock that the communists could over-run if they so wanted.

Troops in Singapore, on the other hand, would at least have a chance (given better leadership than in the Second World War) to fight in any given area from well-equipped headquarters that could not come under quick, direct attack. This was the very reason, of course, why Britain had insisted for decades that she must control the key defence post of Singapore, 'east of Suez', the phrase being borrowed from Rudyard Kipling, who had popularised it in 'Mandalay':

> Ship me somewheres east of Suez
>   where the best is like the worst,
> Where there aren't no Ten Commandments,
>   an' a man can raise a thirst.

It had been known for a year that Britain would *eventually* pull her troops out of Singapore. It had been made clear in a White Paper on Defence, published in July the previous year (1967), but Wilson had specifically mentioned in a Commons debate that his government intended to withdraw 'by the mid seventies', and this was generally interpreted as meaning by 1977. To Lee this meant a breathing space – not to organise defence against a possible aggressor, but to stabilise the unemployment problem that would inevitably follow the closing of the bases. Then, with the devaluation of sterling, the British Government panicked. Almost without warning – and only a few months after promising Lee Kuan Yew his breathing space – the date was brought forward.

Politically the decision to leave troops in Hong Kong while withdrawing them from Singapore seemed incomprehensible. If Britain was so poor that it had to economise, why leave troops in the affluent, booming island of Hong Kong (where a colonial power could jail any possible communists at will) and decide to take them away from the struggling little island of Singapore where unemployment would provide a heaven-sent opportunity for fellow travellers to foment unrest and foster the communist cause?

For the sudden withdrawal of the British presence in Singapore could have created a disastrous vacuum. British bases occupied a tenth of the island. They provided a fifth of the national income. They earned £50 million a year for the Singapore Government in foreign exchange. Most important of all, they were Singapore's biggest employers.

Nearly fifty thousand civilians worked for the British forces. As many more depended upon them because they worked for Service families or lived in satellites of the bases. If all were thrown out of work when the British left, unemployment in Singapore could rise to some two hundred thousand, a tenth of the island's population, and enough to cause serious economic and political problems.

And even ignoring moral issues, for one could argue that charity begins at home (if one also ignored Hong Kong) it seemed such folly to ditch the only leader in Asia willing to back up his commitment to hold fast against communism. The confrontation with Sukarno was barely ended. The Americans were on the verge of losing the Vietnam War; alone among Asian politicians, Lee Kuan Yew stood firm. Politically, he was a friend worth helping.

Even Labour MPs like Sir Dingle Foot, a former Solicitor-General, accused his own party of a breach of faith in South-East Asia and urged Britain to remain until the countries concerned could provide for their own defence; while Desmond Donnelly resigned the Labour Whip, describing the withdrawal as 'betraying promises to associates overseas'.

Lee's first reactions had been predictably angry. It was open to Singapore, he said, to retaliate by withdrawing a substantial part of its sterling balances from London, by inviting Japan to take over the dockyard and by placing shipping, insurance and banking business in countries other than the United Kingdom. He had flown to London for the Commons debate, but his anger soon cooled, for a curious reason which incidentally may account for much of his success. Though he may understand the mentality, the 'philosophy' of the Chinese and other Asians, and though he has fought passionately for the independence of Singapore, in many ways Lee Kuan Yew is as English as roast beef and Yorkshire pudding. His childhood, his youth, his studies were all motivated to make him more English than the English. He is that rare phenomenon, a world statesman of another colour who actually *likes* the English. And this means that he can understand their points of view – and he did over the bases, once his anger was spent. A realist, he returned to Singapore apparently in a happier frame of mind, for he was able to announce that Britain had agreed to leave behind a radar air defence centre, together with associated communications systems, and qualified staff to train local personnel. He also said that Britain had offered Singapore a squadron of Lightning fighters and that he was considering acquiring a missile system. Britain would also give Singapore and Malaysia £75 million in military aid over the following five years to offset the effects of British withdrawal.

Without delay Lee set about the mammoth task of finding uses for the bases, creating new jobs to replace those that would be lost – and all at double speed. In a way the dynamism and pragmatism with which Lee Kuan Yew tackled 'the bases problem' and turned it from disaster into a success story beyond anyone's wildest dreams is symptomatic of everything that has happened as Singapore strode forward to its present position.

British plans for withdrawal went ahead. On 8 December 1968, the Royal Naval dockyard, estimated to be worth £12 million, was formally handed over as a gift to the Singapore Government. (It was, by coincidence, the 27th anniversary of the Japanese landings in Malaya.)

It was accepted by the Singapore Foreign Minister, Mr S. Rajaratnam, who said: 'An imperial heritage can be made to work for the enrichment and progress of our country. For the UK there will also be the satisfaction of knowing that their hundred and fifty years of varied endeavours in Singapore did not all vanish like a puff of smoke.'

He then, in turn, handed over the dockyard to the Sembawang Shipyard (Private) Ltd, the Singapore Government firm formed with £6 million capital to operate the yard for commercial shipyard repair, with Swan Hunter International as managing agents. Hon Sui Sen, its chairman, announced plans to build a second dry dock to take ships of up to 300,000 tons deadweight, which would be half-financed out of British government aid. With a twinge of sadness, Vice-Admiral W. D.

O'Brien, Commander of the Far East Fleet, said, 'It would be quite wrong of me to infer that we in the Royal Navy and the civilian services that support us, rejoice in this event.' Then the national anthems played, a plaque was unveiled, and a young Singapore apprentice broke out the new company's flag. The handover was complete.

The problem facing Singapore fell into two categories – firstly, what to do with military installations, such as missile sites and ammunition depots; and secondly, how best to utilise sites concerned with the servicing and repairs of products – anything from aircraft to watches. Some £1.25 million was earmarked for the conversion of the naval dockyards to commercial use. Other allocations went towards adapting the army vehicle repair centre and turning the RAF base at Changi, with its sickening memories of Japanese brutality, into a holiday camp.

A Bases Economic Conversion Department was set up to map the military areas and suggest uses for them, after which foreign investors were invited to come and inspect them, with priority given to British firms until the withdrawal, after which facilities would be granted on a first come, first served basis.

British businessmen flew to Singapore under the auspices of the Confederation of British Industry, even though in some ways Singapore was not at the time an appealing prospect. (For one thing, it was only 800 miles from the bombs of Vietnam.) But Lee produced inducements to appeal to businessmen that more than offset the drawbacks. Recognising that Singapore could never survive with British-style union practices, he pushed through laws which increased the basic working week to 44 hours and reduced the union voice in management. School leavers who would normally have followed their parents into shopkeeping or clerking were encouraged to train as engineers and technicians. The government channelled millions into building roads, clearing factory sites and expanding power and water supplies. To attract tourists 25 major hotels were planned.

But above all, Singapore offered comparatively low

costs, coupled with easy access to Asian markets. It was already trading with 68 countries, including both North and South Vietnam. Soon it acquired capital transferred from Hong Kong after anti-British demonstrations there, and from Indonesia after a series of violent anti-Chinese riots.

Foreign investment increased. Advertisements placed in the financial press of London and New York proclaimed, 'Singapore is where it's happening.' By the end of the 1960s Singapore had two dozen foreign banks and was bidding to become a financial centre rivalling Tokyo and Hong Kong. By 1970 there were 40 manufacturers in Singapore classed by the government as British, half of them fully owned by Britons. Their products ranged from margarine (Lever Brothers) to foam rubber (Dunlop). Other countries were moving in – like America's Santa Fe Pomeroy, a company making oil storage tanks. The Japanese were arriving with their yen. The Russians opened a branch of the Narodny Bank, the first Russian bank in Asia.

The old barracks, which so many British soldiers had occupied, were torn down and tower blocks erected on sites already piped for water and electricity and linked by roadways. It was as though 'the bases problem' stirred almost everyone in Singapore to an awareness that, in the words of Lee, 'There is no problem we cannot lick, given the will to work together.'

Housing provided one of the most dramatic success stories, for the city's housing improved beyond recognition with a new unit of housing being completed every 45 minutes at one time. By filling swamps and reclaiming land from the sea, Singapore made space for twenty-storey buildings, resettling about half of its population (whether or not they wanted it) in a campaign that made the island the public housing laboratory of the world.

Though the British moved out their troops with almost unseemly speed, the British presence as such did not finally disappear until 30 March 1976, when Colonel J. C. A. Swynnerton, seven officers and men packed their bags at the Equatorial Hotel and made their way to the airport to fly home. And even then a solitary staff sergeant remained until mid-April to settle outstanding bills.

It was the end of the presence that had begun with Raffles, and it marked a watershed in the history of Britain as a world power.

Once the 'disaster' had been put into perspective, the raw material of the bases – a self-contained city – gave the Singapore Government a magnificent opportunity to enlarge and diversify its industry; but that opportunity had to be grasped quickly in order to forestall unemployment. Lee was able to do this because the government had already evolved a pragmatic approach to unemployment, housing, social services – all of which had had to be built up after independence. One example of the basic planning and thinking behind such planning – how the corporate brain ticked, so to speak – is Jurong, for though no one can deny that it is basically a huge, industrial complex devoted to manufacturing, it is also brazen enough to offer tourist attractions, as impertinent as though Cleveland in Ohio or Barnsley in Yorkshire started advertising themselves as holiday resorts.

The development of Jurong, which lies on nearly seven thousand acres of reclaimed swampland and barren hills started in 1961. Today, with a population of seventy thousand workers in more than five hundred factories, it is regarded as something of an economic miracle – largely because it was envisaged as a whole, as a self-contained development for pleasure as well as work, before it ever left the drawing board stage; so that it has everything from its own sewage plant to Singapore's only drive-in cinema. It is ruthlessly zoned for industries, business, residential estates, parks and recreational grounds.

Its factories turn out plywood, electric cables, ceramics, paper products, steel tubes and tyres. There are oil refineries, ship building and repairing yards, car assembly plants, while the Jurong marine base acts as a supply terminal for the offshore oil exploration industry in South-

East Asia. But, however worthy this may be – and it is the reason for the existence of Jurong – it is fascinating to see how, on such a small island as Singapore, Lee Kuan Yew and his men exercised the same care and attention as Raffles and Farquhar did when discussing the layout of the city's first streets.

It is grouped round Jurong Park, which is extraordinary in itself, for it incorporates three artificial islands built on a lake. The park contains not only a golf course, but a Japanese garden covering twenty acres – one of the largest Japanese gardens in the world outside Japan – and an equally large Chinese garden on the lakeside, built along the banks where less than twenty years ago only prawn ponds existed. And this is not all. Jurong Bird Park is the pride of all Singaporeans. Covering nearly forty acres of natural terrain, it is claimed to be the largest bird paradise in the world, and houses over five thousand birds from all continents. Planned by experts from the London Zoological Society – the 'descendants' of its founder Raffles – all the aviaries are designed to resemble the natural environment of the species, the main highlight being a flight-free aviary; a huge netted enclosure where visitors can step in and view the birds at close range. But what a nerve to 'waste' forty acres in the industrial zone of an island the size of Wight!

If all this sounds like a publicity hand-out, one thing should be borne in mind: Jurong is a perfect example of Lee's unshakeable belief that good work and steady wages are not enough alone to prevent men and women from being tempted into communism. Full stomachs, lack of tension and fears for the future do help; but monotony breeds discontent; and monotony is the hallmark of the twentieth century's mechanised workforce. People must be happy in their surroundings, and above all have some pride in their achievements and those they can see around them; one can add a rider to this. Those achievements – and their consequent comforts – must in some way be related to a man's past. Men need to be reassured at every turn. A man working in an expanding, dreary 'new town', living in the prison-like efficiency of a tower block, must be allowed to walk, literally, down memory lane which was a country heath when he was young; or if he was a city boy, down the back alleys. When people refuse to leave their slums, it is not because they love them; it is because they had such good times (or think they did) in 'the good old days'.

But a Chinese loves his links with the past just as much as an East Ender. For decades every Chinese who came to Singapore had only one dream: to go home to China to die. Lee's own grandfather realised just that dream. Today's Singaporeans, mostly of Chinese origin who venerate the past, must keep some links, however tenuous, with that past. Hence the Bird Park at Jurong. It was not erected as a gimmick by some publicity-hunting city planner. The Chinese are among the world's greatest lovers of birds, and the park is crowded every weekend not with tourists but with Chinese workers and their families who return time and again, drawn by a subtle combination of past and present.

The same studied determination not to break too brusquely with the past as the country marches into the future lay behind another remarkable development, the Peoples' Park. Lee knew, when this was first mooted, that you cannot force people to change their ways of life too drastically. The rich Chinese may buy their groceries at the Cold Storage or Robinson's, and dine at Goodwood Park or Raffles, but you cannot force the humble Chinese to buy his groceries at a cut-price supermarket or lunch in a vast impersonal café where no one knows his neighbour.

The Chinese love the tiny shop restaurants, to live their lives among the same groups of people, and this was never lost sight of in the planning of Peoples' Park, an extraordinary slum clearance scheme by any standards.

For eighty years, until 1965, Peoples' Park was an area of Singapore just outside the city centre which teemed with eating stalls, shops, garages, metal workers – a real flea market – all housed in rickety shacks with corrugated iron roofs. If anyone wanted anything in the city then

Peoples' Park was the place to go. And they went by their thousands over the years.

It was colourful if unhygienic, and of course in the end it had to go in the name of 'progress' – just as Covent Garden in London and the equally colourful 'Les Halles' market in Paris had to be replaced by dreary suburban markets. So the government decided to eradicate this 'blemish' on the new-look Singapore.

Starting in 1965, the whole area, which included part of old Chinatown, was torn down. Private contractors were invited to erect a new Peoples' Park, offices and shops. But there were restrictions. The old food stalls were demolished, but a sense of continuity was maintained by barring all boutique-like shops on the ground level where the old shophouses had once served customers who would live in the flats above. Instead, the old food stalls were resited in the new buildings and today the same families still operate the stalls (though in modern conditions) with a history of food stall operation going back a hundred years. The food stalls are tiny – because the Chinese like them that way – and most of them give out on to walkway streets.

Surrounding them, and the flats, are not only tiny shops and restaurants, but Chinese emporiums with goods from Red China at knockdown prices. There are cinemas, laundries, temples, doctors and dentists – in fact everything a man needs within a few yards of his home, yet somehow there is nothing impersonal about Peoples' Park. It differs fundamentally from, say, the magnificent *mercato* of Caracas, or the shopping market of New York's Rockefeller Plaza, and the reason for the difference is not hard to find. The Caracas *mercato* and the New York shopping plaza are for buying and selling. Peoples' Park is for *living* in. It is actually inhabited after dusk.

Many were sorry to see the old Peoples' Park disappear and today all that remains of the old area is the Great Southern Hotel, a splendid old Chinese building, which seems to stand like a sentry at the entrance to the new additions.

16. Today and Tomorrow

To the old Singapore hand returning after a long absence, the visual change that will most startle him lies in the housing estates *outside* Singapore city – tall, utilitarian blocks of flats that somehow look incongruous near palm trees or banana and sago plantations. In this age one expects skyscrapers in even the most unlikely cities – from Monte Carlo to Seoul – but few can deny that the 'brilliant' planners who first foisted these vertical prisons on people as an alternative to slum living took no account of human feelings. There can be few more depressing fates than for a mother with a clutch of children to be rehoused on the friendless twentieth storey of a tower block.

But as in Hong Kong, Singapore faced, as it will always face, a desperate shortage of land. Every inch counts, and so the only solution to the housing problem has been to build upwards. By 1980 three-quarters of the island's population will live in government built high-rise flats. Inevitably high-rise housing brings problems – such as vandalism and suicides; not merely because of the soulless nature of these flats (their effect on the occupants is incalculable) but because they provide an easy way to commit suicide. Most of Singapore's suicide victims now end their lives by jumping from high-rise blocks.

Among the oddest 'victims' of high-rise flats are fishermen who used to live on the island of Sentosa just off the Singapore coast. As tourism boomed, it was decided to turn Sentosa – only three miles long, less than a mile wide – into a major tourist attraction. The few fishermen who lived there were shifted in 1972 to high-rise accommodation on the main island (and must lead puzzled lives). Today a ferry leaves every fifteen minutes to transport tourists from Singapore to Sentosa; or you can go above the narrow strip of water by cable car, to tour the little island in open-sided buses, augmented by a few ex-London double deckers, for cars are not permitted. There is a golf course reclaimed from mangrove swamp, with a remarkable second hole on a coral reef, joined to the land by a bridge, and a deer park and a crocodile farm. As an extra attraction, there is also a waxwork tableau of the British surrender to General Yamashita – quite a draw for Japanese tourists.

But these are trimmings – and nothing, really, can change Singapore. Those who love it are determined never to leave it, among them 'Buck' and Lucy Buckeridge. Buck is now over seventy, Lucy ten years younger, and when Buck retired from the fire brigade in 1957 he and Lucy took a trip round the world for the express purpose of choosing the ideal country in which to retire. They never found a country they liked better than Singapore, so they returned, and will stay in Singapore for the rest of their lives. Lucy Buckeridge, who helped so many penniless evacuees with cash loans during the war, left Robinson's when Buck retired, but in 1960 the firm's chief accountant died suddenly, and Robinson's begged her to help out for three months until they could find a replacement. Lucy said she would – and has remained at Robinson's ever since.

T. W. Ong is still one of Singapore's foremost barristers – though a year or two ago he had to undergo major surgery as a direct result of the continual beatings in the stomach and intestines he suffered when the Japanese suspected him of being a British spy. But after a long illness he recovered and now practises as vigorously as ever.

George Hammonds not only stayed in Singapore but took up Singaporean nationality, and, until he died in 1976, looked upon the city as his real home, and felt that the only proper course to take was to become a citizen of the city and country he had chosen and loved.

No one can tell what the future holds. Singapore's

polyglot population now numbers 2.25 million, of which the biggest proportion (1.7 million) is Chinese. There are also 339,000 Malays and 155,000 Indians. (Many still help to maintain families in their home countries, just like the earliest settlers. Every month Singaporeans remit, quite legally, about $20 million of earned income overseas, mostly to China, India, Pakistan to support aged parents and relatives.) And the population is still growing. It is estimated that by 2030 Singapore will have 3.5 million inhabitants, for Singapore is a country of the young: more than half the people are under twenty-one, and in this lies a great hope. Yet even Lee Kuan Yew will not commit himself to the long distance view. When, early in 1977, he was asked if he was worried about the foreseeable future, he replied, 'The word "foreseeable" depends whether you're long-sighted or short-sighted. I'm not worried for the security of Singapore for the next five to ten years. I would not like to put on a pair of binoculars and go beyond, say, then.'

Though Singapore has, of course, changed with the years, it is still a delight to the senses – to the eyes, the nose, the taste – for it is still a mixture of big bustling city and tropical island. From the moment the weary traveller leaves the airport and drives down the spotless, flower-decked boulevards to the centre of the city, it is a joy.

To someone like myself, who lived there in the 'Somerset Maugham' days, and who has returned year after year, the new skyscraper hotels, the widened avenues, still cannot quite disguise the Singapore of old, nor hide the world of yesterday in a city of tomorrow. I know of no other city that evokes the same nostalgia as Singapore. Every corner is touched with glimpses of the past, as though one is turning the pages of a photograph album and suddenly finds an unexpected old sepia print, long forgotten. Nothing can change the silhouette of the harbour, festooned with the masts of junks, alive with bobbing sampans, the offshore islands barely glimpsed in the shimmering haze of heat. Nothing can ever change the hot sun interrupted by sudden blinding rain, at times so savage that one can hardly drive a car through it.

In Raffles Place the shops may have changed, but the shape has not. Robinson's was burned down some years ago and has now been reborn in Orchard Road. Change Alley is still as boisterous a bargain centre as it was when David Marshall's father opened his shop there, but it has been extended so that, though the old Change Alley is unchanged, when you walk through it and reach Collyer Quay, facing the sea, you can continue walking upwards and onwards. You climb some steps into 'Change Alley of the Air' which crosses the whole main thoroughfare – a street in itself lined with small shops – ending in a vast Chinese restaurant overlooking the harbour.

Raffles Hotel is still – well, Raffles. Its corridors boast a few more boutiques and there is a pool in the garden, but the 90-foot-tall fan-shaped travellers' palms, the hibiscus and frangipani still beckon anyone in search of Maugham – and the best Singapore gin sling on the island at the long bar near the Palm Court where Maugham wrote much of *The Moon and Sixpence* and Conrad conceived *Lord Jim*.

The centre of tourist shopping has moved – it started to move after Robinson's was burned down – from Raffles Place to Orchard Road, where most of the new hotels have been built, with, sandwiched between them, the tiny second-hand shops where the bargains, alas, are no longer bargains.

What was once called 'white Singapore' – the cluster of imposing white government buildings, protective or forbidding according to one's conscience – is unchanged, and so are the streets, for though many have been widened, Victoria Street, Balmoral Road, Orchard Road all provide a comforting touch of nostalgia.

Across from the government buildings lies the *padang* where Sir Shenton Thomas and his European population assembled before the Japanese marched them off to internment in Changi. At one end, looking rather rustic, is the Cricket Club, always a wonderful oasis, but better now, for its multi-racial membership has made it more colourful.

Just off Orchard Road a sentry (in a different kind of uniform) stands guard at the ornate gates of the old Government House, still there, with the same long dining room where Lady Thomas sheltered under the table from Japanese bombs and shells. One wing of the building is now used as the Prime Minister's office, the other as a suite for important visitors – a kind of Singapore Blair House – but to the eye of the old Singapore hand, returning to evoke the past, nothing seems to have changed. The same trees still dot the vast green, carefully manicured lawns that slope towards the gates, the city, its taxis, its raucous trishaw driver who has replaced the rickshaw wallah, the skinny Chinese with a sweatband round the neck, whose job in a short life was to burst his lungs pulling his more fortunate brethren and sisters around Singapore; 'the human donkey', one historian called him.

But old habits die hard and the ghost of the rickshaw still haunts Singapore in the shape of the trishaw, which still gives some tourists an uneasy sense of guilt as they sit back and are transported by a Chinese pedalling the bicycle that pulls them along. Legs, however, seem to last longer than lungs, and many trishaw riders are in their sixties.

The older trishaw hands start their day at 5 am, carrying goods (which don't complain like passengers) from vendors to markets, and then carrying elderly housewives and their packages on their rounds of the same markets. Others – the lucky ones – have 'contracts' for months, taking children between home and school for a fraction of the amount a taxi driver would charge. The newer, younger, brasher breed of trishaw riders prefer to wait for tourists in the Orchard Road area, and decorate their vehicles with neon bulbs, small fans, even small transistor radios. Today there are only about a thousand trishaws in Singapore, compared with nine thousand twenty years ago – possibly because in the same period the cost of buying a trishaw has risen from $120 to $600, a large sum to lay out for a man who can expect on average to earn only $12 a day.

The most vociferous trishaw rank at night is on the edge of an extraordinary patch of land on Orchard Road. If it were ever empty it would resemble nothing so much as a demolition site awaiting a new construction gang. Maybe it is that – only it is never empty. By day it serves as a car park, always filled. But the park closes at 6 pm, and at dusk – any time between 6.20 and 6.30 pm – it miraculously changes into Singapore's largest, noisiest, cheapest, open air restaurant complex. It really *is* extraordinary, the metamorphosis that takes place in a matter of minutes. As the last cars pull out, the stall owners appear. With the deftness of magicians, tables are unfolded, coalpots filled with charcoal, strips of meat and vegetables prepared; lights start to sizzle, coconuts are split, pineapples sliced, and before long the place is jammed with stalls selling anything from a glass of coconut milk to portions of *satay*, pieces of meat grilled Malayan style on thin spindles of wood, no thicker than darning needles, and dipped into a special sauce before you pull them straight off the stick with your teeth.

By day a taxi – and Singapore taxis are surely among the cheapest in the world – will take you out of town, bowling along the Bukit Timah Road, still with orchids growing on its central reservation, past the green lawns of 'Bukit Rose', the house that T. W. Ong's grandfather bought long before 'T.W.' and Lee Kuan Yew worked in the same solicitor's office, and up towards Changi, not only past the infamous jail with its terrible memories, but to blinding white beaches, lined with bending palms, or twisted mangroves, their writhing, evil-looking branches still unchanged from the day when Stamford Raffles landed on its shores in January 1819, and changed the destiny of this magical island in the sun.

Selected List of Books Consulted

Backhouse, Sally, *Singapore* (David & Charles, 1972)

Braddell, Roland, *The Lights of Singapore* (Methuen, 1934)

Buchanan, Iain, *Singapore in Southeast Asia* (G. Bell, 1972)

Buckley, Charles Burton, *An Anecdotal History of Old Times in Singapore*, 2 vols (Fraser & Neave, 1902)

Cameron, John, *Our Possessions in Malayan India* (Smith, Elder & Co., 1865)

Chapman, F. Spencer, *The Jungle Is Neutral* (Chatto & Windus, 1949)

Collis, Maurice, *Raffles* (Faber & Faber, 1966)

Cook, J. A. Bethune, *Sir Thomas Stamford Raffles* (Arthur H. Stockwell, 1918)

Coupland, R., *Raffles* (Oxford University Press, 1926)

George, T. J. S., *Lee Kuan Yew's Singapore* (Andre Deutsch, 1973)

Hahn, Emily, *Raffles of Singapore* (Doubleday & Co., 1946)

Kirby, S. Woodburn and others, *The War against Japan*, 5 vols (HMSO, 1957–69)

Lawrence, Anthony, *Foreign Correspondent* (Allen & Unwin, 1972)

McKie, R. C. H., *This Was Singapore* (Robert Hale, 1950)

Makepeace, W., Brooke, G. E. & Braddell, R. St J., *One Hundred Years of Singapore*, 2 vols (John Murray, 1921)

Marks, Harry J., *The First Contest for Singapore 1819–24* (Martinus Nijhoff, 1959)

O'Ballance, Edgar, *Malaya: The Communist Insurgent War 1948–60* (Faber & Faber, 1966)

Winstedt, Richard, *Britain and Malaya 1786–1941* (Longman Green, 1944)

Acknowledgements

The author and publishers are most grateful to Ray K. Tyers for kind permission to reproduce photographs previously published in the two volumes of his book *Singapore Then and Now* (University Education Press, Singapore, 1976). Thanks are due to him for all the photographs reproduced here, except for the following: portrait of Raffles (by courtesy of the National Portrait Gallery, London), the German Club in 1900 (Singapore National Archives), Goodwood Park Hotel (R. M. Brooker Ltd), street barbers in Orchard Road today (New Nation Publishing, Singapore), Lee Kuan Yew (Popperphoto).

Index